AP WORLD HISTORY PRACTICE EXAMS

SPARK
NOTES

SPARK PUBLISHING

Practice exams and explanations written by David Clarke.
Study cards written by Sharon Cohen.
SparkCharts written by Mark Engler and Margaret Welles.

Spark Publishing
120 Fifth Avenue
New York, NY 10011
www.sparknotes.com

ISBN-13: 978-1-4114-0486-1
ISBN-10: 1-4114-0486-6

Please submit changes or report errors to www.sparknotes.com/errors

Printed and bound in China.

CONTENTS

ACKNOWLEDGMENTS

SparkNotes would like to thank the following writers and contributors:

Dave Clarke
AP World History teacher, Nathan Hale High School, West Allis, Wisconsin

Sharon Cohen
AP World History teacher, Springbrook High School, Silver Spring, Maryland;
AP World History exam development committee member

J. Victor Ortiz
AP World History teacher, Verdugo Hills High School (LAUSD), Tujunga, California

INTRODUCTION

If you're looking at this book, you're probably at least considering taking the Advanced Placement World History Exam. And there are many good reasons to do so: AP exams give you the opportunity to earn valuable course credit or advanced standing in college as well as the opportunity to impress on college admissions officers that you are a serious and dedicated student. AP exams offer one of the few chances to *prove* to colleges that you are already capable of doing college-level work.

In fact, the AP exams have become so highly touted, surrounded by so many expectations about what they say about you and what they can do for you, that it's easy for you to become overwhelmed or intimidated. We're here to tell you that the AP World History Exam is manageable. We're here to help.

Practice exams are one of the best ways to study for AP exams because they take away some of the mystique and hype regarding the exams and allow you to get comfortable with what's actually on the test. More important, they can help you understand what's *not* on the exam, so you don't waste your time striving for some elusive ideal of "college-level preparation." Practice exams will help you see the test as it really is, so you know exactly what to expect.

Before launching right into the exams, we'll give you an overview of how the test is structured and precisely what kinds of questions you'll see on it.

FORMAT OF THE EXAM

The Advanced Placement World History Exam is 3 hours and 5 minutes long and is divided into two parts:

- A 55-minute multiple-choice section, which counts for 50 percent of your score
- A 130-minute free-response section, which counts for 50 percent of your score

The Multiple-Choice Section

Format

Section I of the exam contains 70 multiple-choice questions, which you are given 55 minutes to complete. The questions test your knowledge of material usually covered in a college introductory world history course.

The multiple-choice questions are either questions or incomplete statements, followed by five suggested answers or completions. The exam graders penalize you a quarter-point for each wrong answer, so you should guess only if you can eliminate two or more of the answer choices.

Topics of Questions

The multiple-choice questions on the World History Exam can be grouped in two ways. The first is chronologically. All multiple-choice questions will fall into one of the following five eras:

- 8,000 B.C.E. to 600 C.E.
- 600 C.E. to 1450
- 1450 to 1750
- 1750 to 1914
- 1914 to the present

Each of the above eras accounts for roughly the same percentage of questions on the exam. In other words, you will see roughly 14 questions from each era. If any period is given more emphasis, it will be the period 600 C.E. to 1450, which may account for two or three more test questions than the other eras.

The second way to group the multiple-choice questions on the AP World History Exam is by theme. Each question will fall into one of the following topics:

- **Patterns and Impacts of Interactions.** This theme addresses how societies interact, currently and historically, through trade, war, diplomacy, and international organizations.
- **Relationship of Change and Continuity.** Questions regarding how people and societies have either changed or remained the same over time will fall into this category.
- **Impact of Technology and Demography.** This theme examines the effects that technology and population change have had on people and the environment, including topics such as disease, manufacturing, migrations, agriculture, and weaponry.
- **Social and Gender Structure.** Questions falling into this category address the characteristic features of individual societies, how those features have changed over time, and how interactions with differing societies have allowed for change.
- **Cultural and Intellectual Developments.** Questions regarding cultural advancements, including art, literature, and writing systems fall into this category.
- **Changes in Functions and Structures of States.** This theme looks at the development of a political culture in societies, including political organizations, modern forms of government, and citizens' interaction with and relationship to government.

As in the chronological categories, each of these themes is equally represented on the AP World History Exam, with roughly 14 questions on each theme. If there is any particular emphasis, it will be on the **Patterns and Impacts of Interactions** theme and the **Changes in Functions and Structures of States** theme.

The Free-Response Section

Types of Questions

Section II of the exam is a 130-minute free-response section broken into three parts:

- **Part A, The DBQ.** Part A consists of one document-based essay question (DBQ). This question will usually focus on a specific time period and requires that the student both analyze and interpret the documents provided as well as apply his or her own knowledge of the time period to construct a coherent essay. The student will most likely not be familiar with the documents, which will include charts, graphs, cartoons, pictures, and articles. Part A begins with a required 10-minute reading period in which students analyze the documents and plan their answer. Students then have 40 minutes to write their response.
- **Part B, The "Change over Time" essay.** Part B consists of one standard essay question addressing a "change over time." This question will ask the student to examine a society and describe its evolution over at least one time period. Students will have 40 minutes to plan and write their response.
- **Part C, The Comparison essay.** Part C consists of one standard essay question addressing a broad comparison between at least two societies. Students will have 40 minutes to plan and write their answer.

Scoring

In the free-response section, each of the three essays counts for one-third of your total Section II score. Each essay is scored on a scale from 1 to 9:

8–9	High Score
6–7	Medium-High Score
5	Medium Score
3–4	Medium-Low Score
1–2	Low Score

Answers to the questions in this section will be judged on the strength of the thesis developed and quality of the argument rather than on factual information. For example if you incorrectly identify the date of a battle in the Boer War in one of your essays, you will not be penalized. A sample essay and specific scoring information for each question in Section II of the exam is covered in the Answers & Explanations section of each exam in this book.

SCORING

The AP World History Exam is scored on a five-point scale:

5	Extremely well qualified
4	Well qualified
3	Qualified
2	Possibly qualified
1	No recommendation

HOW TO PREPARE FOR THE EXAM

The AP World History Exam not only tests your knowledge of facts but also your ability to analyze a set of facts and draw conclusions. These skills are tested in both sections of the test and are by far the most important skills you need to get a high score. In other words, it's not enough that you know the dates of the major battles in the Civil War. You have to understand why the Battle of Gettysburg was so crucial to the outcome of the war and to the future of the United States. Dates and other facts are important, but the AP graders are more concerned with how you pull all that information together.

This is a skill that you can improve. The best way is to take a lot of practice tests. That's why we've included two full-length tests in this book. The more familiar you are with analysis questions the better you'll be able to handle them. While some multiple-choice questions will ask you to analyze a set of facts and draw conclusions, these skills will primarily be tested in the free-response section of the exam. The more practice you have developing quality thesis statements and supporting arguments in a timed essay format, the better off you'll be on test day.

STRATEGIES FOR TAKING THE EXAM

Multiple Choice

- Skim the questions first so you know what kind of information the questions are asking you to provide.
- Answer the questions you feel confident with first, skipping harder questions and saving them for last.
- Guess on questions when you can eliminate at least two wrong answers.
- Mark the questions you can't answer with a check—tackle all of these questions after you've gone through all of Section I.
- Cross off wrong answers on your test itself.

Free Response

- Read the prompt carefully, underlining and marking the key parts of the question.
- Brainstorm ideas for your thesis and the evidence you will use to support it.
- Outline your essay in the form of a thesis supported by reasons and evidence.
- Reread the prompt to make sure you haven't missed part of the question.
- Don't get hung up on perfect wording, spelling, etc.
- Don't get upset if you can't remember exact dates or names, because you won't be penalized for that in this section.
- If you run out of time, at least try to put down an outline of what you would like to have written for the essay. You won't get full credit, but you may be able to pick up a point or two.

REGISTERING FOR THE EXAM

Contact your school's AP coordinator or guidance counselor for help registering for the test. If you are homeschooled or your school does not administer the test, contact AP Services for information about registering to take the exam at another school in your area.

AP Services

P.O. Box 6671

Princeton, NJ 08541-6671

(888) CALL-4-AP; (609) 771-7300

TTY: (609) 882-4118

email: apexams@ets.org

website: www.collegeboard.com/ap/students/

PRACTICE EXAM 1

AP WORLD HISTORY PRACTICE EXAM 1 ANSWER SHEET

1. Ⓐ Ⓑ Ⓒ Ⓓ Ⓔ	19. Ⓐ Ⓑ Ⓒ Ⓓ Ⓔ	37. Ⓐ Ⓑ Ⓒ Ⓓ Ⓔ	55. Ⓐ Ⓑ Ⓒ Ⓓ Ⓔ
2. Ⓐ Ⓑ Ⓒ Ⓓ Ⓔ	20. Ⓐ Ⓑ Ⓒ Ⓓ Ⓔ	38. Ⓐ Ⓑ Ⓒ Ⓓ Ⓔ	56. Ⓐ Ⓑ Ⓒ Ⓓ Ⓔ
3. Ⓐ Ⓑ Ⓒ Ⓓ Ⓔ	21. Ⓐ Ⓑ Ⓒ Ⓓ Ⓔ	39. Ⓐ Ⓑ Ⓒ Ⓓ Ⓔ	57. Ⓐ Ⓑ Ⓒ Ⓓ Ⓔ
4. Ⓐ Ⓑ Ⓒ Ⓓ Ⓔ	22. Ⓐ Ⓑ Ⓒ Ⓓ Ⓔ	40. Ⓐ Ⓑ Ⓒ Ⓓ Ⓔ	58. Ⓐ Ⓑ Ⓒ Ⓓ Ⓔ
5. Ⓐ Ⓑ Ⓒ Ⓓ Ⓔ	23. Ⓐ Ⓑ Ⓒ Ⓓ Ⓔ	41. Ⓐ Ⓑ Ⓒ Ⓓ Ⓔ	59. Ⓐ Ⓑ Ⓒ Ⓓ Ⓔ
6. Ⓐ Ⓑ Ⓒ Ⓓ Ⓔ	24. Ⓐ Ⓑ Ⓒ Ⓓ Ⓔ	42. Ⓐ Ⓑ Ⓒ Ⓓ Ⓔ	60. Ⓐ Ⓑ Ⓒ Ⓓ Ⓔ
7. Ⓐ Ⓑ Ⓒ Ⓓ Ⓔ	25. Ⓐ Ⓑ Ⓒ Ⓓ Ⓔ	43. Ⓐ Ⓑ Ⓒ Ⓓ Ⓔ	61. Ⓐ Ⓑ Ⓒ Ⓓ Ⓔ
8. Ⓐ Ⓑ Ⓒ Ⓓ Ⓔ	26. Ⓐ Ⓑ Ⓒ Ⓓ Ⓔ	44. Ⓐ Ⓑ Ⓒ Ⓓ Ⓔ	62. Ⓐ Ⓑ Ⓒ Ⓓ Ⓔ
9. Ⓐ Ⓑ Ⓒ Ⓓ Ⓔ	27. Ⓐ Ⓑ Ⓒ Ⓓ Ⓔ	45. Ⓐ Ⓑ Ⓒ Ⓓ Ⓔ	63. Ⓐ Ⓑ Ⓒ Ⓓ Ⓔ
10. Ⓐ Ⓑ Ⓒ Ⓓ Ⓔ	28. Ⓐ Ⓑ Ⓒ Ⓓ Ⓔ	46. Ⓐ Ⓑ Ⓒ Ⓓ Ⓔ	64. Ⓐ Ⓑ Ⓒ Ⓓ Ⓔ
11. Ⓐ Ⓑ Ⓒ Ⓓ Ⓔ	29. Ⓐ Ⓑ Ⓒ Ⓓ Ⓔ	47. Ⓐ Ⓑ Ⓒ Ⓓ Ⓔ	65. Ⓐ Ⓑ Ⓒ Ⓓ Ⓔ
12. Ⓐ Ⓑ Ⓒ Ⓓ Ⓔ	30. Ⓐ Ⓑ Ⓒ Ⓓ Ⓔ	48. Ⓐ Ⓑ Ⓒ Ⓓ Ⓔ	66. Ⓐ Ⓑ Ⓒ Ⓓ Ⓔ
13. Ⓐ Ⓑ Ⓒ Ⓓ Ⓔ	31. Ⓐ Ⓑ Ⓒ Ⓓ Ⓔ	49. Ⓐ Ⓑ Ⓒ Ⓓ Ⓔ	67. Ⓐ Ⓑ Ⓒ Ⓓ Ⓔ
14. Ⓐ Ⓑ Ⓒ Ⓓ Ⓔ	32. Ⓐ Ⓑ Ⓒ Ⓓ Ⓔ	50. Ⓐ Ⓑ Ⓒ Ⓓ Ⓔ	68. Ⓐ Ⓑ Ⓒ Ⓓ Ⓔ
15. Ⓐ Ⓑ Ⓒ Ⓓ Ⓔ	33. Ⓐ Ⓑ Ⓒ Ⓓ Ⓔ	51. Ⓐ Ⓑ Ⓒ Ⓓ Ⓔ	69. Ⓐ Ⓑ Ⓒ Ⓓ Ⓔ
16. Ⓐ Ⓑ Ⓒ Ⓓ Ⓔ	34. Ⓐ Ⓑ Ⓒ Ⓓ Ⓔ	52. Ⓐ Ⓑ Ⓒ Ⓓ Ⓔ	70. Ⓐ Ⓑ Ⓒ Ⓓ Ⓔ
17. Ⓐ Ⓑ Ⓒ Ⓓ Ⓔ	35. Ⓐ Ⓑ Ⓒ Ⓓ Ⓔ	53. Ⓐ Ⓑ Ⓒ Ⓓ Ⓔ	
18. Ⓐ Ⓑ Ⓒ Ⓓ Ⓔ	36. Ⓐ Ⓑ Ⓒ Ⓓ Ⓔ	54. Ⓐ Ⓑ Ⓒ Ⓓ Ⓔ	

AP WORLD HISTORY

Three hours and 5 minutes are allotted for this examination: 55 minutes for Section I, which consists of multiple-choice questions, and 2 hours and 10 minutes for Section II, which consists of essay questions. 10 minutes of Section II are devoted to a mandatory reading period, primarily for the document-based essay question in Part A. Section I is printed in this examination booklet. Section II is printed in a separate booklet. In determining your grade, the two sections are given equal weight.

SECTION I

Time—55 minutes
Number of questions—70
Percent of total grade—50

Section I of this examination contains 70 multiple-choice questions. Therefore, please be careful to fill in only the ovals that are preceded by numbers 1 through 70 on your answer sheet.

General Instructions

INDICATE ALL YOUR ANSWERS TO QUESTIONS IN SECTION I ON THE SEPARATE ANSWER SHEET. No credit will be given for anything written in this examination booklet, but you may use the booklet for notes or scratchwork. After you have decided which of the suggested answers is best, COMPLETELY fill in the corresponding oval on the answer sheet. Give only one answer to each question. If you change an answer, be sure that the previous mark is erased completely.

Example: Sample Answer

    Chicago is a   Ⓐ Ⓑ Ⓒ ● Ⓔ

        (A) state
        (B) continent
        (C) country
        (D) city
        (E) village

Many candidates wonder whether or not to guess the answers to questions about which they are not certain. In this section of the examination, as a correction for haphazard guessing, one-fourth of the number of questions you answer incorrectly will be subtracted from the number of questions you answer correctly. It is improbable, therefore, that mere guessing will improve your score significantly; it may even lower your score, and it does take time. If, however, you are not sure of the best answer but have some knowledge of the question and are able to eliminate one or more of the answer choices as wrong, your chance of getting the right answer is improved, and it may be to your advantage to answer such a question.

Use your time effectively, working as rapidly as you can without losing accuracy. Do not spend too much time on questions that are too difficult. Go on to other questions and come back to the difficult ones later if you have time. It is not expected that everyone will be able to answer all the multiple-choice questions.

AP WORLD HISTORY
SECTION I: MULTIPLE-CHOICE QUESTIONS
Time—55 minutes
70 Questions

Directions: Each of the questions or incomplete statements below is followed by five suggested answers or completions. Select the one that is best in each case and then fill in the corresponding oval on the answer sheet.

Note: This examination uses the chronological designations B.C.E. (before the Common Era) and C.E. (Common Era). These labels correspond to B.C. (before Christ) and A.D. (anno Domini), which are used in some world history textbooks.

I.   II.   III.

1. Which of the following correctly matches the symbols above to their respective religions?

    (A) I. Hinduism   II. Judaism   III. Confucianism
    (B) I. Buddhism   II. Islam   III. Daoism
    (C) I. Buddhism   II. Judaism   III. Confucianism
    (D) I. Daoism   II. Islam   III. Buddhism
    (E) I. Daoism   II. Christianity III. Hinduism

2. Which of the following is true of both Asoka and Constantine? Both

    (A) extended their empires farther than ever before
    (B) presided over the final days of their empires
    (C) established new policies governing the conduct of merchants
    (D) came to power through political intrigues, including assassination
    (E) advocated little-known religions, after military victories

3. The caste system of India includes all of the following EXCEPT

    (A) a caste of kings and rulers
    (B) a caste of women
    (C) a caste of farmers and businessmen
    (D) a caste of priests
    (E) a caste of laborers

4. Which of the following is an accurate description of Islam, Buddhism, and Christianity? Each

    (A) featured a strong missionary movement
    (B) was born during the Axial Age, c. 800–200 B.C.E.
    (C) embraces the idea of reincarnation
    (D) was founded in or around the Fertile Crescent
    (E) holds merchants in very low status

5. Which of the following products were frequently traded across the Sahara Desert in the period 600 to1450?

    (A) Salt, ivory, gold, cloth
    (B) Salt, guns, porcelain, silk
    (C) Silk, horses, spices, sugar
    (D) Coffee, gold, diamonds, silk
    (E) Ivory, cloth, guns, wine

6. "We Mongols believe that there is but one God, by Whom we live, and by Whom we die, and toward Him we have an upright heart. But just as God gives different fingers to the hand, so has He given different ways to men."

    —Mongke Khan, as witnessed by William of Rubuck, a Franciscan Friar, who met Mongke Khan

    What Mongol attitude or policy does the above quote best reflect?

    (A) The determination of the Mongols to eliminate polytheism
    (B) The animistic nature of the traditional Mongolian religion
    (C) The Mongol preference toward monotheistic religions like Islam
    (D) The religious tolerance of Mongols toward other peoples
    (E) The frequent conversion of Mongols to Tibetan Buddhism

GO ON TO THE NEXT PAGE

AP WORLD HISTORY MULTIPLE-CHOICE QUESTIONS

7. Which of the following best explains why Chinese porcelain and Indian cotton were frequently found in East Africa, in the period 600 C.E. to 1450?

(A) Chinese explorers established colonies in East Africa as early as 750 C.E.
(B) Indian rulers frequently established cities in East Africa as trade entrepôts.
(C) There was frequent trade carried across the Indian Ocean between Asia and Africa.
(D) Many East Africans traveled to India and China in search of these and other products.
(E) A key trade route ran down the East African coast from Damascus and the Silk Road.

8. Which of the following describes a difference between the Code of Chivalry in feudal Europe and the Code of Bushido in feudal Japan? Chivalry

(A) was adapted in Europe from Arab codes, whereas Bushido was uniquely Japanese
(B) viewed honor as secondary to victory, whereas Bushido valued honor above all else
(C) was a secular, moral code, whereas Bushido was closely tied to Japanese faiths
(D) applied to all men in Europe, whereas Bushido bound only Samurai
(E) viewed women as objects for protection, whereas Bushido did not offer them extra status

9. Which of the following best explains why both Chinese emperors and Turkish sultans had multiple wives and/or concubines? Having multiple wives and/or concubines

(A) was a proscribed duty under the local faith
(B) offered greater possibilities for diplomatic marriages
(C) meant greater economic wealth through large dowries
(D) offered the ruler greater social status
(E) helped insure a male heir to the throne

10. Which of the following were the three Muslim empires established after the collapse of the Ilkhanate?

(A) Ottoman, Mamaluk, and Byzantine
(B) Ottoman, Safavid, and the Sultanate of Delhi
(C) Ottoman, Mughal, and Byzantine
(D) Ottoman, Safavid, and Mughal
(E) Safavid, al-Andalus, and the Sultanate of Delhi

11. Which of the following was true of Islam in the period 600 C.E. to 1450?

(A) Muslim rulers persecuted non-Muslims to force conversions.
(B) Muslim religious scholars released various teachings opposing trade.
(C) Women were given positions of great authority in government.
(D) Cultural unity was supported as people learned Arabic throughout Islamic lands.
(E) The influence of Islam had not yet spread across the Sahara.

12. Which of the following nations' claims to newly discovered lands were separated by the Treaty of Tordesillas in 1495?

(A) Spain and England
(B) Spain and Portugal
(C) England and France
(D) Venice and the Ottoman Empire
(E) China and Portugal

GO ON TO THE NEXT PAGE

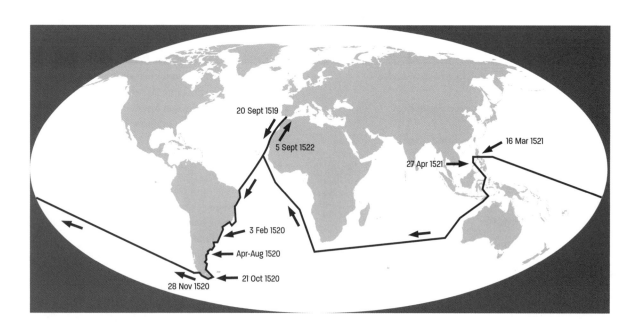

13. Which of the following is shown in the map above?

   (A) The voyages of Vespucci
   (B) The voyages of Zheng He
   (C) The voyages of De Gama
   (D) The four voyages of Columbus
   (E) The voyage of Magellan and his crew

GO ON TO THE NEXT PAGE

AP WORLD HISTORY MULTIPLE-CHOICE QUESTIONS

14. Which of the following products were brought to Europe through the Colombian Exchange?

    (A) Horses and potatoes
    (B) Horses and tobacco
    (C) Potatoes and sheep
    (D) Potatoes and tobacco
    (E) Sugar and tobacco

15. Which of the following describes how Islam's and Christianity's views of slavery were different? Muslims

    (A) were willing to enslave anyone, whereas Christians saw slavery as inherently sinful
    (B) and Christians both opposed slavery on religious grounds
    (C) and Christians would both enslave anyone but would free slaves who converted
    (D) could not enslave fellow Muslims, whereas Christians were open to enslaving any faith
    (E) and Christians were both willing to enslave anyone, regardless of faith

16. Which of the following is an accurate description of the various categories applied to inhabitants of colonial Central and South America? Mulattos were

    (A) part white and part African whereas mestizos were part white and part native
    (B) part white and part native whereas mestizos were part African and part native
    (C) part native and part African whereas mestizos were whites born in the New World
    (D) Africans who had been freed whereas mestizos were whites born in the New World
    (E) natives who worked with the Europeans whereas mestizos were African

17. The impact that guns had on the societies of West Africa was most similar to which of the following?

    (A) The impact of guns on Ming China
    (B) The impact of guns on feudal Japan
    (C) The impact of guns on Mughal India
    (D) The impact of guns on Eastern Africa
    (E) The impact of guns on Central America

GO ON TO THE NEXT PAGE

© Getty Images

18. Hagia Sophia, pictured above, is an example of

(A) the cultural diffusion that occurred between Europe and India
(B) the cultural diffusion that occurred between Catholicism and Eastern Orthodoxy
(C) the cultural diffusion that occurred between India and Egypt
(D) the Persian cultural influence on Jerusalem
(E) the Islamic cultural influence on Istanbul, formerly Constantinople

GO ON TO THE NEXT PAGE

19. Who of the following would be considered an author of the Enlightenment?

   (A) Copernicus
   (B) Karl Marx
   (C) Martin Luther
   (D) Erasmus
   (E) Voltaire

20. Which of the following was a key principle of mercantilism?

   (A) The belief in absolute monarchy
   (B) The importance of increasing a nation's imports
   (C) Having a favorable balance of trade
   (D) The necessity of low tariffs
   (E) Strong government regulation of key industries

21. "Take up the White Man's burden
    Send forth the best ye breed"

    Rudyard Kipling, "The White Man's Burden," 1899

    The phrase above is from a poem encouraging

   (A) Western countries to accept a greater role in liberating slaves
   (B) imperialism of non-Western countries by industrialized nations
   (C) immigration of Europeans to the Americas
   (D) Africans and Asians to fight back against European aggressors
   (E) the export of European livestock to the Americas

22. Both Britain's and Japan's strides toward industrialization

   (A) followed an existing blueprint of modernizing
   (B) began in the eighteenth century
   (C) were only successful because of the will of a powerful monarch
   (D) overcame early opposition from traditional feudal lords who opposed modernization
   (E) benefited early on in the process from an increase in food supply, resulting in an increase of workers for factories

23. Which of the following was a result of the Industrial Revolution?

   (A) Women's rights deteriorated as men became wealthier through investments in industry.
   (B) Urbanization increased, created by workers settling near the factories and mills.
   (C) Trade between Europe and East Asia dwindled, as Europe became more self-sufficient.
   (D) There was an increased reliance on extended families, as factory workers were usually poor.
   (E) Per capita income among citizens of industrialized nations decreased.

24. All the following were once a part of Mexico EXCEPT

   (A) Texas
   (B) Nicaragua
   (C) Panama
   (D) Honduras
   (E) California

25. Which of the following describes an effect of the Industrial Revolution on both industrialized and non-industrialized nations?

   (A) The growing demand for labor required more people to work in agriculture.
   (B) The population of cities declined as artisans moved to jobs in factories.
   (C) Women increasingly joined the workforce to satisfy the needs of the industrial economy.
   (D) The growth of industry forced nations to focus on local needs instead of global trade.
   (E) New fuel sources, such as coal, replaced older sources on an epic scale.

26. Which of the following correctly describes the social hierarchy of the estates of pre-Revolutionary France?

   (A) first, nobility; second, clergy; third, everyone else
   (B) first, clergy; second, nobility; third, everyone else
   (C) first, wealthy; second, middle class; third, poor
   (D) first, King; second, nobility; third, everyone else
   (E) first, clergy; second, nobility; third, merchants; fourth, farmers

GO ON TO THE NEXT PAGE

27. Leaders of the French Revolution were most like the leaders of the American Revolution in which of the following ways?

    (A) They fought extended battles against the military of their king.
    (B) They used execution of enemies and rivals as a tactic for rallying support.
    (C) Their primary objection to their government involved the demand to end colonial rule.
    (D) They were primarily from the middle or upper classes of their societies.
    (E) They were largely motivated by the possibility of self-enrichment.

28. All of the following were leaders of either the French or American Revolution EXCEPT

    (A) Francois Toussaint L'Overture
    (B) Maximillian Robespierre
    (C) Benjamin Franklin
    (D) Thomas Jefferson
    (E) Jean-Paul Marat

29. Which of the following is the best example of a secular government in an Islamic nation of the twentieth century?

    (A) Ayatollah Khomeini's Iran
    (B) Gammal Abdel Nassar's Egypt
    (C) The Taliban in Afghanistan
    (D) Mohammad Khatami-Ardakani's Iran
    (E) The Saud family in Saudi Arabia

30. Which of the following accurately describes a comparison between nations of the developed and developing world?

    (A) Developed—high unemployment; developing—low unemployment
    (B) Developed—high infant mortality; developing—low infant mortality
    (C) Developed—high literacy; developing—low literacy
    (D) Developed—low unemployment; developing—high unemployment
    (E) Developed—low literacy, high per capita income; developing—high literacy

31. Which of the following is the political party that has dominated Mexican government for most of the past century?

    (A) Social Democratic Party (PDS)
    (B) Mexican Green Ecological Party (PVEM)
    (C) Party of the Democratic Revolution (PRD)
    (D) Institutional Revolutionary Party (PRI)
    (E) Mexican Communist Party (PCM)

32. Which of these is known as the Intifada?

    (A) The continuous uprising by Palestinians against Israel since 1987
    (B) The modernization movement among younger, more progressive Iranians
    (C) The prohibition against Islamic dress codes for women by the Turkish government
    (D) The quest for an autonomous Kurdish state in northern Iraq
    (E) The most militant of the Egyptian Islamic political parties

GO ON TO THE NEXT PAGE

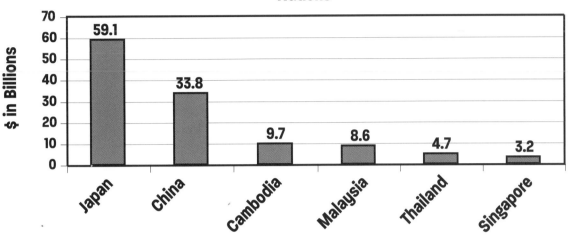

1995 U.S. Trade Deficit with Select Asian Nations

33. The graph above demonstrates which of the following?

(A) The United States has significant trade deficits with one of its most key allies on the Pacific Rim.

(B) Trade between the United States and China has grown at a rapid rate in the last decade.

(C) Japanese electronics makes up the bulk of the imports into the United States.

(D) Nations with democratic governments have better economies than those who do not.

(E) The signing of NAFTA was intended to decrease the United States' foreign debt.

GO ON TO THE NEXT PAGE

AP WORLD HISTORY MULTIPLE-CHOICE QUESTIONS

34. Which of the following nations were members of the European Union by 2004?

    (A) Poland, Latvia, and Croatia
    (B) Ireland, Spain, and Turkey
    (C) Austria, France, and Russia
    (D) Germany, Bulgaria, and Romania
    (E) Finland, Italy, and Hungary

35. Which of the following were characteristic of the Russian and Chinese communist revolutions? Both

    (A) were movements of a small group of citizens against unjust governments
    (B) took place in countries where agriculture was more prevalent than industry
    (C) were proceeded by failed military operations that weakened the ruling party
    (D) took place shortly before global military conflicts
    (E) were movements that triggered extensive U.S. military intervention

36. In the period 8000 B.C.E. to 600 C.E., merchants' position in society was the highest in which empire?

    (A) Tang China
    (B) Han China
    (C) Gupta/Mauryan
    (D) Roman
    (E) Alexander's empire

37. Which of the following represents two of the Five Confucian Relationships?

    (A) Brother and Sister; Landlord and Tenant
    (B) Father and Son; Priest and Religious Faithful
    (C) Employer and Worker; Husband and Wife
    (D) Older and Younger Brother; Landlord and Tenant
    (E) Ruler and Subject; Father and Son

38. Which of the following are characteristic of both Christianity and Judaism?

    (A) Dietary prohibitions against pork and other foods and the monotheistic nature of God
    (B) A belief in the Ten Commandments and the monotheistic nature of God
    (C) Acceptance of Jesus as a prophet and belief in his divinity
    (D) Respect for the covenants with Moses and Noah and the divinity of Jesus
    (E) Resistance to Roman rule leading to persecution and acceptance of the Holy Trinity

39. All of the following were sects within Christianity by 1055 C.E. EXCEPT

    (A) Eastern Orthodoxy
    (B) Catholicism
    (C) Copticism
    (D) Lutheranism
    (E) Nestorianism

GO ON TO THE NEXT PAGE

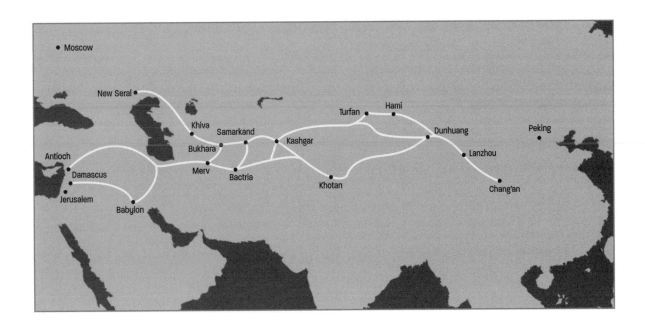

40. The map above demonstrates which of the following about trade on the Silk Road in the period 600 C.E. to 1450?

(A) While many items were traded, the most important item traded was silk.
(B) Trade was dominated throughout its length by the Chinese.
(C) Frequent bandit attacks prevented commerce from going directly from Dunhuang to Kashgar.
(D) Pastoral nomadic traders were more successful merchants than those from settled societies.
(E) Trade involved China as well as Central and Western Asia.

GO ON TO THE NEXT PAGE

41. All of the following are among the Five Pillars of Islam EXCEPT

    (A) ritual bathing before prayer
    (B) fasting during daylight of the holy month
    (C) pilgrimage to Mecca, if possible
    (D) recitation of faith in Allah and Muhammad
    (E) daily prayers recited facing Mecca

42. Which of the following was true of both Mongol yurts and the teepees of some Native Americans?

    (A) They were transportable and made mostly of animal hides.
    (B) They were constructed to face the morning sun in the east.
    (C) Size indicated the relative importance of the occupant.
    (D) Remains of these permanent dwellings can still be found today.
    (E) They were left open at the top for ceremonial and religious reasons.

43. "By the mid-twelfth century, even before the general revival of Ptolemy in Europe, when the Arab geographer Al-Idrisi made his world map in 1150 for Roger II, Norman King of Sicily, he too used a grid scheme which, like that on Chinese maps, makes no allowance for a curved earth. Perhaps, as Joseph Needham suggests, the long tradition of grid maps of China had reached the Arabs in Sicily through the Arab colony at Canton and through the increasing number of Arab travelers to the East. And so perhaps the Chinese played a part in ending the Great Interruption— setting European geographers once again on the path of knowledge, rediscovering the quantitative tools that were the heritage of Greece and Rome."

    Daniel J. Boorstein, *The Discoverers*

    Another navigational development that would support the passage above was

    (A) the invention of the astrolabe by Venetian merchants
    (B) the development of the geometry of spheres by Muslim mathematicians
    (C) the diffusion of the compass from China to Europe
    (D) the diffusion of astronomical charts from Europe to China
    (E) the development of lateen sails by Muslims

44. Which of the following best explains why some Native Americans were eager to assist Cortez in his attacks on the Aztecs?

    (A) The Aztecs required tribute in goods, and sometimes persons, from conquered peoples.
    (B) The Aztec kings had recently raised land taxes to the extent that many farmers were starving.
    (C) Aztec armies regularly pressed rural villages for new recruits, siphoning off young men.
    (D) Native customs required that any and all assistance be granted to strangers asking help.
    (E) Spanish horses frightened the natives more than fighting the Aztecs did.

45. Which of the following was a traveler most like Marco Polo?

    (A) Salah al-Din (Saladin)
    (B) Mansa Musa
    (C) Moses Maimonides
    (D) Omar Khay'yam
    (E) Ibn Battuta

GO ON TO THE NEXT PAGE

© Keystone/Getty Images

46. The type of boat pictured above enabled the Vikings to do which of the following?

   (A) Make detailed copies of such a craft using an alphabet derived from Greek
   (B) Sail up and down major rivers, raiding and trading as far as Constantinople and Paris
   (C) Carry large amounts of captured treasure below decks for transit
   (D) Turn the boats over on shore to create makeshift shelters
   (E) Round the West African coast to reach as far south as the Niger River delta

GO ON TO THE NEXT PAGE

47. Which of the following is true of both the Bantu and Germanic migrations?

   (A) They both contributed to the fall of the Roman Empire in the fifth century.
   (B) They both emigrated from the Central Asian steppes.
   (C) They both displaced some local inhabitants and brought different cultures and traditions to the regions they encountered.
   (D) Their knowledge of bronze made them formidable opponents.
   (E) Farming of wheat and fishing made up the bulk of their diets during migrations.

48. Which of the following occurred during the early Renaissance (fourteenth century) and enabled Europeans to begin to develop a sense of national identity?

   (A) The fall of Constantinople
   (B) The independence movement of the Netherlands
   (C) The Mongol invasions
   (D) The split of the Church into Eastern and Western factions
   (E) The Hundred Years War between France and England

49. All of the following explain why the islands of Southeast Asia include Indian, Islamic, Dutch, and Chinese cultural elements EXCEPT

   (A) the region served as a point where Chinese and Japanese goods were exchanged for Indian goods
   (B) straits and other geographic features made control of trade by "outsiders" relatively easy
   (C) merchants in search of spices and other goods settled there while acquiring these products
   (D) local rulers often offered refuge to immigrants unwelcome in their home countries
   (E) monsoon winds blew across the Indian Ocean to the islands for half the year

50. In which of the following ways was the encomienda system of the Spanish New World like the feudal system of Medieval Europe?

   (A) Resident farmers were considered part of the land and could be bought and sold with it.
   (B) Encomienda land owners had authority to knight former conquistadors.
   (C) Encomienda landowners were sovereign, never answering to anyone else.
   (D) Lands were subdivided among nobles, who divided it among the local farmers.
   (E) Pressure from members of the Church also brought an end to the feudal system.

51. Which of the following women was not the ruler of a major nation between 1450 and 1750?

   (A) Elizabeth I of England
   (B) Marie-Therese of Austria
   (C) Dowager Cixi of China
   (D) Isabella of Castile
   (E) Nzinga of Matamba

52. Which of the following describes a way in which the Ottoman Empire was different from the Safavid Persian Empire?

   (A) The Ottoman Empire was largely land based whereas the Safavid power was not bound by the sea.
   (B) The Ottomans were Sunni Muslims whereas the Safavids were Shi'ite.
   (C) The Ottoman Empire, even at its height, was considerably smaller than the Safavid.
   (D) A sultan ruled the Ottoman Empire, whereas a cadre of clerics ruled the Safavid.
   (E) The Ottoman Empire survived the Mongol invasions whereas the Safavid did not.

53. Which of the following was a result of European Atlantic trade with Africa?

   (A) Africans began to boycott Muslim goods from Egypt.
   (B) Trade centers shifted from trans-Saharan to Atlantic coastal trade routes.
   (C) Merchant contacts with Africa enabled diseases to be spread back to Europe.
   (D) The influx of African gold led to severe inflation in Europe.
   (E) Europeans introduced slavery to Africa.

GO ON TO THE NEXT PAGE

54. "As soon as the coin in the coffer rings, the soul from purgatory springs."

Johann Tetzel, c. 1517

Which of the following was an objection of Martin Luther's to Church teaching and reflected in the quote above?

(A) Mass and the Bible were only to be in Latin, not translated into local languages.
(B) Priests were often charged to perform rites or sacraments, such as baptisms.
(C) Salvation was considered to be gained through good works alone.
(D) Clergy members were allowed to accumulate great wealth.
(E) Forgiveness for sins could be received in return for donations to the Church.

55. In which of the following ways were Louis XIV of France and Aurangazeb of the Mughal Empire similar? Both

(A) had great military success but were intolerant of religions other than their own
(B) revived the economies of their nations through global trade on the Indian Ocean
(C) improved the status of women and slaves in their societies
(D) tried to create syncretic religions and assimilate conquered peoples
(E) fought major battles against the Ottoman Empire

56. Which of the following were key naval battles that affected the futures of major empires in the period 1450 to 1750?

(A) The Battle of Lepanto and the Battle of the Nile
(B) The Battle of Agincourt and the Battle of the Nile
(C) The defeat of the Armada and the Battle of Lepanto
(D) The Battle of Waterloo and the Battle of Diu
(E) The Manzikert and the defeat of the Aztecs under Montezuma

57. In which of the following cities did the Qing dynasty confine European merchants starting around 1760?

(A) Beijing
(B) Nanjing
(C) Shanghai
(D) Macao
(E) Guangzhou

58. In which of the following ways were French and English colonies in the Americas different?

(A) The French sent only Catholics whereas the English also sent Puritans.
(B) The French were most interested in establishing colonies whereas the English only wanted furs.
(C) Most French colonists were men whereas the English sent whole families as colonists.
(D) Colonies had little impact on the French economy but were vital to the economy of England.
(E) Relations between the English and natives were hostile whereas the French co-existed peacefully with the natives.

59. Which of the following led several revolutions in nations of Central and South America?

(A) Simon Bolivar
(B) Francois Toussiant L'Overture
(C) Bartolome De Las Casas
(D) Miguel Hidalgo
(E) Napoleon Bonaparte

60. "Manifest destiny" can best be described as which of the following?

(A) The belief among Americans that God wished the nation to expand to the Pacific
(B) The theory that Native Americans were incapable of self-government
(C) A theory that sought to explain the economic fluctuations in American trade
(D) The belief among nationalistic Mexicans that Texas was vital to the survival of Mexico
(E) A philosophy that predicted the ultimate triumph of Christianity over all other faiths

GO ON TO THE NEXT PAGE

61. Which of the following describes both the Boxer Rebellion and the Indian National Congress?

   (A) The goal of both was to get the English out of India.
   (B) Both sought to create native monarchies in place of European rule.
   (C) Each was eventually put down by Western military power.
   (D) Neither was successful due to poor leadership.
   (E) Each was a nationalist movement against Western powers.

62. Which of the following accurately describes both the Seven Years' War and the Boer War?

   (A) They each pit British forces against other European colonial forces.
   (B) They were fought on more than one continent.
   (C) Both led to the expansion of Dutch territory.
   (D) Each was a conflict between a European power and a colonized people.
   (E) Both were primarily religious wars at heart.

63. What did America's policy of Dollar Diplomacy accomplish in the early 1900s?

   (A) It kept the U.S. dollar tied to the gold standard.
   (B) It bought the goodwill of other countries through extensive foreign aid to poorer nations.
   (C) It allowed for the peaceful acquisition of territories like Alaska and the Gadsden Purchase.
   (D) It led to U.S. intervention in Latin America to protect local American investments.
   (E) It allowed for the increase of exports and high tariffs to improve trade balance.

GO ON TO THE NEXT PAGE

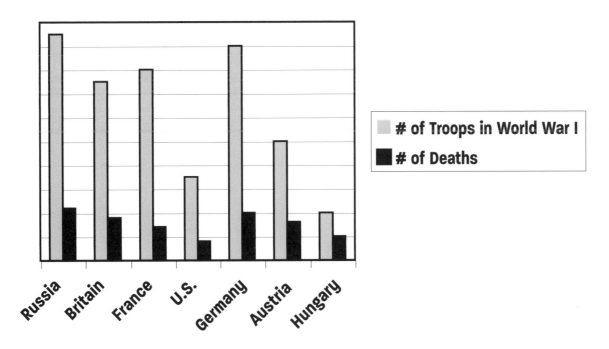

64. Which of the following can be seen from the graph above?

(A) The greatest number of deaths was among the Central Powers.
(B) The highest ratio of deaths to number of troops was the British.
(C) Those nations that were governed by monarchs suffered less than democracies.
(D) The nations who declared war latest suffered the fewest deaths.
(E) Those nations with the most advanced militaries suffered more deaths than those with older militaries.

GO ON TO THE NEXT PAGE

65. All of the following are problems faced by modern sub-Saharan nations of Africa EXCEPT

(A) civil wars caused by colonial borders that grouped rival ethnicities in the same country
(B) a lack of democratic history or participatory government structures
(C) an unequal distribution of population between rural and urban areas
(D) the spread of AIDS and other health crises untreated by local or national governments
(E) indebtedness to developed nations through the IMF and World Bank

66. Which of the following was a major advancement in women's rights that occurred in the 1910s to the 1920s?

(A) The League of Nations issued an International Declaration of Women's Rights.
(B) India officially outlawed sati.
(C) Women in many industrial nations received the right to vote.
(D) Women in Islamic nations acquired the legal right to divorce.
(E) The Catholic Church began to ordain women as priests.

67. In which of the following ways were Muhammad Ali Jinnah and Mohandas Gandhi similar?

(A) Both were Muslims from the Gujarat region of India.
(B) They advocated nonviolence in the cause of revolution.
(C) They are both celebrated as national heroes in Pakistan.
(D) Both worked for the independence of their nation from Britain.
(E) They worked together to divide British India into three separate parts.

68. Which of the following statements about twentieth-century revolutions is true?

(A) Revolutions never give more rights to women, as women are generally more reactionary.
(B) All revolutions must originate in the upper class to have any success.
(C) All revolutions, at their core, are about economic issues.
(D) All revolutions were in some way connected to Marxism.
(E) Most revolutions support rights for women to encourage them to join the cause.

69. All of the following were nations that experienced some form of genocide in the twentieth century EXCEPT

(A) Cambodia
(B) the Soviet Union
(C) Nicaragua
(D) Nazi Germany
(E) Rwanda

70. "The third balance that you have to pay attention to in the globalization system—the one that is really the newest of all—is the balance between individuals and nation-states. Because globalization has brought down many of the walls that limited the movement and reach of people and because it has simultaneously wired the world into networks, it gives more power to individuals to influence both markets and nation-states than at any time in history."

Thomas L. Friedman. *The Lexus and the Olive Tree*. New York: Anchor Books, 2000: p. 14

Which of the following might be considered an example that supports the quote above?

(A) Aung San Su Kyi and Osama bin Laden
(B) Kim Jong Il and the Catholic Church
(C) General Electric and Juan Peron
(D) the United States and Japan
(E) the *New York Times* and the Al Jazeera Network

END OF SECTION I

AP WORLD HISTORY
SECTION II

You will have 10 minutes to read Section II. You are advised to spend most of the 10 minutes analyzing the documents and planning your answer for the document-based question in Part A. If you have time, you may spend some portion of the time reading the questions in Part B and Part C. At the end of the 10 minutes, you may begin writing your answers. Suggested writing time is 40 minutes for the document-based essay question in Part A. You will have 5 minutes of planning time and 35 minutes of writing time for each essay question in Part B and Part C.

BE SURE TO MANAGE YOUR TIME CAREFULLY

Note: This examination uses the chronological designations B.C.E. (before the common era) and C.E. (common era). These labels correspond to B.C. (before Christ) and A.D. (anno Domini), which are used in some world history textbooks.

Part A
(Suggested writing time—40 minutes)
Percent of Section II score—33 $\frac{1}{3}$

Directions: The following question is based on the accompanying Documents 1 through 8. (The documents have been edited for the purpose of this excercise.)

This question is designed to test your ability to work with and understand historical documents. Write an essay that:

- has a relevant thesis that is supported by evidence from the documents
- uses all or all but one of the documents
- analyzes the documents by grouping them in as many appropriate ways as possible. **Do not simply summarize the documents individually.**
- takes into account both the sources of the documents and the authors' points of view

You may refer to relevant historical information not mentioned in the documents.

1. Using the documents, discuss the attitudes of ancient Greece and China toward the individual in society. Consider the different roles of people in each society. What kinds of additional documents would you need to assess the affects of these attitudes on society?

Document 1

Source: Edith Hamilton. *Mythology.*

The Greeks had made their gods in their own image. That had not entered the mind of man before. Until then, gods had had no semblance of reality. They were unlike all living things. . . . The storyteller found Hermes among the people he passed in the street.

He said the god "like a young man at that age when youth is loveliest," as Homer says. . . . He was the fulfillment of their search for beauty. They had no wish to create some fantasy shaped in their own minds. All the art and all the thought of Greece centered in human beings.

GO ON TO THE NEXT PAGE

Document 2

Source: Plutarch. *The Life of Theseus,* c. 110 C.E.

Now, after the death of his father Aigeos, forming in his mind a great and wonderful design, [Theseus] gathered together all the inhabitants of Attica [a region near Athens] into one town, and made them one people of one city, whereas before they lived dispersed, and were not easy to assemble upon any affair for the common interest.

Nay, differences and even wars often occurred between them, which he by his persuasions appeased, going from township to township, and from tribe to tribe. And those of a more private and mean condition readily embracing such good advice, to those of greater power he promised a commonwealth without monarchy—a democracy, or people's government—in which he should only be continued as their commander in war and the protector of their laws, all things else being equally distributed among them; and by this means brought a part of them over to his proposal.

Document 3

Source: Eva March Tappan, ed. *The World's Story: A History of the World in Story, Song, and Art, Volume I: China, Japan, and the Islands of the Pacific.*

Besides worship in presence of the representative tablet, periodical rites are performed at the family cemetery. In spring and autumn, when the mildness of the air is such as to invite excursions, city families are wont to choose a day for visiting the resting places of their dead. Clearing away the grass and covering the tombs with a layer of fresh earth, they present offerings and perform acts of worship. This done, they pass the rest of the day in enjoying the scenery of the country.

Document 4

Source: Thucydides (c.460/455–c.399 B.C.E.): Pericles' Funeral Oration from *History of The Peloponnesian War*.

Our constitution does not copy the laws of neighboring states; we are rather a pattern to others than imitators ourselves. Its administration favors the many instead of the few; this is why it is called a democracy. If we look to the laws, they afford equal justice to all in their private differences; if no social standing, advancement in public life falls to reputation for capacity, class considerations not being allowed to interfere with merit; nor again does poverty bar the way, if a man is able to serve the state, he is not hindered by the obscurity of his condition. The freedom which we enjoy in our government extends also to our ordinary life.

Document 5

Source: Confucius. *The Analects.* c. 500 C.E.

Chi K'ang-tzu asked Confucius about government, saying, "What do you say to killing unprincipled people for the sake of principled people?" Confucius replied, "Sir, in carrying on your government, why should you use killing at all? Let your evinced desires be for what is good, and the people will be good. The relation between superiors (ch'n-tzu) and inferiors is like that between the wind and the grass. The grass must bend, when the wind blows across it."

GO ON TO THE NEXT PAGE

Document 6

Source: Han Fei-tzu (d. 233 B.C.E.). *Legalist Views on Good Government*.

But the wisdom of the people is useless: They have the minds of little infants! If an infant's head is not shaved, its sores will spread, and if its boil is not opened, it will become sicker. Yet while its head is being shaved and its boil opened, one person has to hold it tight so that the caring mother can perform the operation, and it screams and wails without end. Infants and children don't understand that the small pain they have to suffer now will bring great benefit later.

Document 7

Source: Richard E. Nisbett. *The Geography of Thought*.

The holism common to [Taoism, Confucianism and Buddhism] suggested that every event is related to every other event. A key idea is the notion of resonance. If you pluck a string on an instrument, you produce a resonance in another string. Man, heaven, and earth create *resonances* in each other. If the emperor does something wrong, it throws the universe out of kilter.

Document 8

Source: J.B. Bury and Russell Meiggs. *A History of Greece*.

[In ancient Greece,] [t]he fighting is done, and the victory won, by regiments of mailed foot-lancers, who march and fight together in close ranks. The secret had been discovered that the well-drilled phalanx of hoplites, as they were called, was superior to the aristocratic method of fighting on horse....Every well-to-do citizen could now provide himself with an outfit of armor and go forth to battle in panoply. The transformation was distinctly leveling and democratic; for it placed the noble and the ordinary citizen on an equality in the field.

END OF PART A

GO ON TO THE NEXT PAGE

AP WORLD HISTORY
SECTION II
Part B

(Suggested planning and writing time—40 minutes)
Percent of Section II score—33 $\frac{1}{3}$

Directions: You are to answer the following question. You should spend 5 minutes organizing or outlining each essay. Write an essay that:

- has a relevant thesis and supports that thesis with appropriate historical evidence
- addresses all parts of the question
- uses historical context to show change over time and/or continuities

2. Choose ONE of the areas listed below and analyze how each area was affected or influenced by colonialism from 1750 to the present. Be sure to include the area's role in global patterns of political and economic behavior in your answer.

   - India
   - Central America
   - North Africa
   - The Middle East

GO ON TO THE NEXT PAGE

AP WORLD HISTORY
SECTION II
Part C

(Suggested planning and writing time—40 minutes)
Percent of Section II score—33 $\frac{1}{3}$

Directions: You are to answer the following question. You should spend 5 minutes organizing or outlining each essay. Write an essay that:

- has a relevant thesis and supports that thesis with appropriate historical evidence
- addresses all parts of the question
- makes direct, relevant comparisons

3. Cities were an important part of the expanding world trade in the period 600 to 1450. Discuss the major similarities and differences between two of the following cities, involving their economic as well as non-economic characteristics:

- Guangzhou
- Timbuktu
- Venice
- Baghdad

WHEN YOU FINISH WRITING, CHECK YOUR WORK ON SECTION II IF TIME PERMITS.

END OF EXAMINATION

PRACTICE EXAM 1: ANSWERS & EXPLANATIONS

Answer Key for Practice Exam 1

Number	Answer	Right	Wrong	Number	Answer	Right	Wrong	Number	Answer	Right	Wrong
1	B	___	___	25	C	___	___	49	D	___	___
2	E	___	___	26	B	___	___	50	A	___	___
3	B	___	___	27	D	___	___	51	C	___	___
4	A	___	___	28	A	___	___	52	B	___	___
5	A	___	___	29	B	___	___	53	B	___	___
6	D	___	___	30	C	___	___	54	E	___	___
7	C	___	___	31	D	___	___	55	A	___	___
8	E	___	___	32	A	___	___	56	C	___	___
9	E	___	___	33	A	___	___	57	E	___	___
10	D	___	___	34	E	___	___	58	E	___	___
11	D	___	___	35	B	___	___	59	A	___	___
12	B	___	___	36	C	___	___	60	A	___	___
13	E	___	___	37	E	___	___	61	E	___	___
14	D	___	___	38	B	___	___	62	A	___	___
15	D	___	___	39	D	___	___	63	D	___	___
16	A	___	___	40	E	___	___	64	D	___	___
17	B	___	___	41	A	___	___	65	C	___	___
18	E	___	___	42	A	___	___	66	C	___	___
19	E	___	___	43	C	___	___	67	D	___	___
20	C	___	___	44	A	___	___	68	E	___	___
21	B	___	___	45	E	___	___	69	C	___	___
22	E	___	___	46	B	___	___	70	A	___	___
23	B	___	___	47	C	___	___				
24	C	___	___	48	E	___	___				

HOW TO CALCULATE YOUR SCORE

Section I: Multiple Choice

$$[\underline{\hspace{2cm}} - (\tfrac{1}{4} \times \underline{\hspace{2cm}})] \times 0.8571 = \underline{\hspace{2cm}}$$

Number
Correct
(out of 70)

Number Wrong

Weighted
Section I Score
(Do not round.)

Section II: Free Response

Question 1 $\underline{\hspace{2cm}}$ $\times$ 2.2222 $=$ $\underline{\hspace{2cm}}$
(out of 9)

Question 2 $\underline{\hspace{2cm}}$ $\times$ 2.2222 $=$ $\underline{\hspace{2cm}}$
(out of 9)

Question 3 $\underline{\hspace{2cm}}$ $\times$ 2.2222 $=$ $\underline{\hspace{2cm}}$
(out of 9)

Sum $=$ $\underline{\hspace{2cm}}$

Weighted
Section II Score
(Do not round.)

Composite Score

$$\underline{\hspace{2cm}} + \underline{\hspace{2cm}} = \underline{\hspace{2cm}}$$

Weighted Section I
Score

Weighted Section II
Score

Composite Score
(Round to the nearest
whole number.)

Composite Score*	AP Grade	Interpretation
78–120	5	extremely well qualified
62–77	4	well qualified
43–61	3	qualified
27–42	2	possibly qualified
0–26	1	no recommendation

*Each year the Development Committee determines the formulas used to calculate the raw composite scores. The Chief Faculty Consultant determines how the composite scores fit into the 5-point AP scale.

SECTION I: MULTIPLE–CHOICE EXPLANATIONS

1. **B** Cultural and Intellectual Developments: 8000 B.C.E.–600 C.E.
The eight-spoked wheel is the symbol of Buddhism representing the Eightfold Path. The Star and Crescent is the most recognized symbol of Islam, although it has no direct connection to the Prophet or the Qur'an. The tai chi, or yin and yang symbol, represents Daoism (also known as Taoism), as the balance between the forces in life (e.g., dark and light, male and female, night and day).

2. **E** Changes in Functions and Structures of States: 8000 B.C.E.–600 C.E.
Both Asoka and Constantine were rulers of major empires (Maurya and Rome, respectively). Both were also victorious in military battles, which apparently changed their views of the world. Asoka converted to Buddhism after viewing the carnage of a battle and became a great advocate for the then-fledgling religion, even sending his own children as missionaries to Sri Lanka. Constantine had a dream or vision that showed a Christian symbol and told him that the symbol would make him victorious. He had his troops put the symbol on their shields and subsequently won the battle. He then converted to Christianity and named it a legal religion in the Roman Empire.

3. **B** Social and Gender Structure: 8000 B.C.E.–600 C.E.
While women have a lower status than men in Hinduism (and generally, in all the world's religions) there is not a separate caste for women. A woman within a particular caste would have less status than a man of equal rank, but more status than a man of lower caste. This is an important concept for understanding how karma and dharma influence reincarnation.

4. **A** Impact of Technology and Demography: 8000 B.C.E.–600 C.E.
This question draws on the student's understanding of the spread of religions. All three faiths were zealous in their missionary activity; Islam's influence stretched as far as Spain and East Asia, whereas Buddhism extended from Egypt to Japan. Christianity spread throughout the world, especially during the voyages of the Age of Discovery. However, only Buddhism was born during the Axial Age (answer choice **B**), with Christianity (c. 33 C.E., the death of Christ) and Islam (622 C.E., the Prophet's hijra) being much later. Of the three, only Buddhism espouses reincarnation in any form (answer choice **C**). Buddhism was also founded in India, far from the Fertile Crescent (answer choice **D**). Finally, Buddhism expresses no view, good or bad, regarding merchants (answer choice **E**). At times, Christianity has looked down on certain forms of trade; because the Prophet was himself a merchant, it is a respected profession in Islam.

5. **A** Patterns and Impacts of Interaction: 600 C.E.–1450
This question requires students to note the time period and the region. Trans-Saharan trade is widely associated with salt, gold, ivory, and manufactured goods such as cloth. While guns (answer choice **B**) were an important import into West Africa, they were not a key commodity during this period. Porcelain, silks, and spices, along with sugar and coffee, were important trade goods in the world trading systems, but primarily in the Indian Ocean or on overland trade routes, not in West Africa. Diamonds are a current export of modern West Africa, but were not a significant part of the trade of the period. Wine was likewise a frequent trade item in Europe, but not across the Sahara.

6.   **D**   Cultural and Intellectual Developments: 600 C.E.–1450

Compared to other political entities of their day, the Mongols were very tolerant of the religious beliefs of others. While many did convert to Islam (answer choice **C**), many did not. Many converted to Tibetan Buddhism (answer choice **C**), and many others remained faithful to the traditional animistic religion of the steppes (answer choice **B**). However, the quote reflects the tolerance of the Khan, not Mongol tendencies toward conversions. There is no suggestion of eliminating any faith (answer choice **A**).

7.   **C**   Patterns and Impacts of Interaction: 600 C.E.–1450

Trade across the Indian Ocean was extremely important and lucrative in this era. Monsoon winds blew ships toward East Africa for half the year, and then blew ships back toward the Pacific the other half of the year. However, neither China nor India ever claimed any part of Africa as part of their political sphere. Likewise, East Africans did not frequently sail as far as India or China, because merchants were blown to them instead. While these goods might have been found on the Silk Road, and while trade might have occurred over land to North Africa, the best explanation of how these goods would end up in East Africa is **C**.

8.   **E**   Social and Gender Structure: 600 C.E.–1450

Specifically defining either of these codes can be difficult because both were developed as romantic nostalgia after the feudal ages. Both, however, had close ties to the values of Christianity (Chivalry) and Buddhism and Confucianism (Bushido). Both viewed the warrior's honor as greater than anything else (except loyalty, and perhaps service to God, in the case of knights). Also, both were locally developed, with no more outside influence than might have come with the settlement of Europe by Germanic peoples or the cultural diffusion that brought Confucianism and Buddhism to Japan in the first place. In each case, only the warrior class was bound by the code. Chivalry however, did exalt women and place them on a pedestal (in theory, at least) while Bushido did not make special allowances for conduct toward women, making answer choice **E** the best choice. In fact, it was possible, though unusual, for the daughter of a samurai to be trained as a warrior.

9.   **E**   Social and Gender Structure: 600 C.E.–1450

European monarchs, like Henry VIII, were forced to rely on the fertility of just one woman or risk running afoul of the Catholic Church. In most other societies, however, having multiple wives and/or concubines was indeed common practice among royalty and the aristocracy. The importance of continuing the family line was seen as too important to entrust to fate, if extra wives could be afforded. While having multiple wives was also a sign of status (because the man could clearly afford to feed and clothe them) the other tangible benefits, as suggested in the other answers, were not a matter of fact. Likewise, as an emperor or sultan, the ruler would not need to obtain greater social status. Neither faith demanded men to take multiple wives, nor were there any economic advantages (answers **A** and **C**). While diplomatic marriages were common in nearly every society, the Chinese and Turkish rulers did not offer their own wives or concubines up for such purposes (answer choice **B**).

10.   **D**   Changes in Functions and Structures of States: 600 C.E.–1450

All of the empires listed were Islamic except the Byzantine Empire (answer choice **A**). The Sultanate of Delhi, choice **B**, was founded in 1192, before the collapse or even creation of the Mongol Ilkhanate. The Mamluk Kingdom of Egypt, choice **A**, also predated the Ilkhanate, as did Al-Andalus, choice **E**. Only choice **D** represents three Muslim kingdoms established after the fall of the Ilkhanate in 1335.

11.   **D**   Cultural and Intellectual Developments: 600 C.E.–1450

Throughout the early history of Islam, forced conversion was extremely rare (choice **A**). Persecutions more often took the form of taxes or fees on non-Muslims or restrictions on religious practices. In many Islamic lands, members of other faiths were allowed to hold high offices. This was not however true of women (choice **C**). Islam encouraged trade, choice **B**, as the Prophet had been a merchant himself, and reached across the Sahara during this period (choice **E**). Kings of Ghana had converted to Islam as early as the tenth century. That leaves choice **D** as the correct answer.

12.   **B**   Patterns and Impacts of Interaction: 1450–1750

The treaty separated the newly claimed lands of Portugal (mostly Africa, the Indian Ocean, and Brazil) from the lands discovered for Spain by Columbus—i.e., the rest of Central and South America (choice **B**). The treaty, created by the pope, established a line at 60˚ west longitude. Everything west of the line went to Spain; east of the line was officially Portuguese. The voyages of Magellan (a Portuguese sailing for the Spanish) were key in the discovery of the Philippines because they established the western limit to Portuguese claims.

13.   **E**   Patterns and Impacts of Interaction: 1450–1750

The map shows the voyages of Magellan and his crew (Magellan himself was killed in the Philippines), as they were the first to circumnavigate the globe. Columbus never left the Atlantic region (choice **D**), while De Gama and Zheng He (choices **B** and **C**) were primarily in the Indian Ocean. Vespucci's trip was also across the Atlantic (choice **A**).

14.   **D**   Patterns and Impacts of Interaction: 1450–1750

Of the products on the list, only potatoes and tobacco (choice **D**) came to Europe through the Colombian Exchange. Horses and sheep were part of the Exchange that went to the New World, from Europe. Sugar (choice **E**) was an import to Europe, but it was not part of the Colombian Exchange. Its origins seem to have been in Southeast Asia, where Muslim merchants encountered it and brought to the Mediterranean region. Europeans grew sugar first on the Atlantic islands off Africa and in (formerly Muslim) Spain.

15.   **D**   Social and Gender Structure: 1450–1750

The religious attitudes of Muslims and Christians are important in understanding the spread of both religions. According to the religious scriptures, Muslims were not to enslave fellow Muslims, although a slave who converted to Islam would not be freed. This explains why many East Africans converted to Islam, as it was a preventative measure against slavery. Christians, however, were under no such restriction. West Africans who converted to Christianity (perhaps aware of the stipulation in Islam and assuming it carried over into Christianity) were gravely mistaken. Slaves who converted to Christianity were not released.

16. **A**   Social and Gender Structure: 1450–1750
The racial divisions among the inhabitants of the Spanish New World were varied and complex. At the top were whites, or *peninsulares,* born in Europe and who had only recently arrived in the Americas. Below them were Creoles, people of solely European extraction who had been born in the New World. Below them, things got murky, as there were numerous combinations possible. Among these were the mestizos who were of both European and native heritage, and mulattos, whose heritage included European and African descendants. This makes answer choice **A** the right answer. At the bottom of the hierarchy were Africans (usually slaves) and the native peoples who had survived the demographic devastation wrought by the arrival of the Europeans. Generations of intermarriage however, enabled many individuals to cross these barriers.

17. **B**   Impact of Technology and Demography: 1450–1750
The arrival of guns in West Africa created what are sometimes referred to as "gunpowder empires." That is, in regions where traditional rivalries existed, the introduction of guns enabled one society to overpower its enemies. This parallels the situation that developed when guns arrived in feudal Japan. Ming China (choice **A**) did not move rapidly to switch to gun technology for a variety of reasons, including the Confucian preference for tradition over innovation. Likewise, Mughal India and East African nations (choices **D** and **E**) did not make extensive use of the European's favorite weapon. While some Native Americans did adopt the gun, these were primarily in North America. Also, it is important to realize that simply having access to guns did not create a "gunpowder empire." Only in cases in which the guns destabilized an existing military balance can the term be applied.

18. **E**   Cultural and Intellectual Developments: 1450–1750
The church of Hagia Sophia was a famous landmark in Byzantine Constantinople. After Constantinople's capture by the Ottoman Turks, the city was renamed Istanbul. This fact alone eliminates most of the possible answers. The cultural influence (note the minarets) was Islamic and Turkish, although the Turkish style borrowed from Persian and Arabic architecture as well.

19. **E**   Cultural and Intellectual Developments: 1450–1750
The Enlightenment refers primarily to the eighteenth century, when Western European thinkers were trying to find scientific principles that applied to society. Smith sought principles of economic behavior, whereas thinkers like Rousseau expounded on the human condition. Given this rough timeframe, choice **A**, Copernicus (1473–1543), choice **D**, Erasmus (1466–1536), and choice **C**, Luther (1483–1546) are all too early. Marx, choice **B**, (1818–1883) is too late. Voltaire (1694–1778) is the only choice in the right time period. Additionally, he was French, as were many other key Enlightenment thinkers.

20. **C**   Patterns and Impacts of Interaction: 1450–1750
Mercantilism was a European economic theory. In short, it sought power for nations through economic strength. Among the sources of this economic strength were gold and silver resources (such as Spanish silver mines in Peru) and favorable balances of trade (choice **C**). One way of improving a nation's balance of trade was to have high tariffs that would discourage imports, not low tariffs, choice **D**. While this theory obviously involved government to play a key role, it was not a role that called for regulation of businesses, choice **E**. Beliefs about monarchy, choice **A**, were not a part of the theory.

21. **B**   Cultural and Intellectual Developments: 1750–1914

Kipling's "White Man's Burden" is one of the most famous poems of the late nineteenth century. Written in response to the Spanish-American War, Kipling appeared to be urging the United States to join Britain (and other European nations) in spreading Western culture to Africa, Asia, and the rest of the Americas. Views such as these served as justifications for European imperialistic attempts all over the world.

22. **E**   Impact of Technology and Demography: 1750–1914

The move toward industrialization, ironically, began on the farm. Britain's population rose dramatically in the early part of the eighteenth century, in part due to an increase in food production, creating a growing population that would become the first generation of factory workers. Japan, in the mid-nineteenth century, also increased food production in order to increase population, just as the British had done a century earlier, making answer choice **E** correct. While there were feudal figures in Japan who resisted modernization, the British government faced no such resistance. Additionally, the strides toward industrialization in Britain were led by parliament, not the king. While Japan closely studied the industrialization and military practices of Britain, Germany, and other industrialized nations, Britain had no such pattern to follow, but had to blaze its own trail.

23. **B**   Impact of Technology and Demography: 1450–1750

The Industrial Revolution (c. 1750) drew on laborers leaving farms to work in factories. Improved agricultural technology required fewer farm workers (and food production continued to increase), and as these workers moved to industrial cities, the size of cities increased, making answer choice **B** the correct choice. Because the average factory worker was not highly paid, women often had to work to support the family. While they were paid less than men, it was a stepping stone to improving women's status in society, eliminating answer choice **A**. Families, however, began to decline in size in cities, as small apartments couldn't house the large extended families common in rural areas, which eliminates answer **D**. While workers were poor, the upper class reaped great rewards. Per capita income actually increased during the Industrial Revolution, deleting choice **E**, although the distribution of wealth was grossly unequal. Trade with the world increased as industrialized nations sought raw materials and markets for their growing stockpiles of merchandise, which eliminates answer choice **C**.

24. **C**   The Relationship of Change and Continuity: 1750–1914

Americans are usually familiar with the war between the United States and Mexico, fought in the 1840s, which made Texas a part of the United States. However, Mexico once stretched much farther to the south. In 1825, the present day nations of Guatemala, Honduras (not to be confused with British Honduras—modern Belize), El Salvador, Costa Rica, and Nicaragua seceded from Mexico, forming the Central American Federation. Having just achieved its independence in 1821, Mexico was unable to prevent their withdrawal. In 1838, the Central American federation broke up into the nations we know today. Panama, answer choice **C**, was the only country listed that was never a part of Mexico. It was, however, once a part of Columbia. Panama became independent in 1903 as part of a deal brokered by a French engineer to have the Panama Canal built by the United States.

25. **C**   Patterns and Impacts of Interaction: 1750–1914

While the Industrial Revolution did have a dramatic impact on both the industrialized and non-industrialized nations of the world, those effects varied greatly. Whereas industrialized nations saw more people moving to work in factories, non-industrialized nations did not have such movement. Thus industrialized nations saw cities grow, making answer choices **A** and **B** incorrect. The increase in manufacturing led to an increase in global trade, including a demand for raw materials from non-industrialized nations (answer **D**). However, whereas industrialized nations switched to coal, coke, and other forms of fuel, the technology for doing so was not transferred to non-industrialized nations (choice **E**), except in specific circumstances (e.g., British railways in India). Women worldwide, however, saw their lives impacted greatly, making answer choice **C** correct. Women in industrialized cities went to work in factories, while women in non-industrialized nations had their labor transferred from traditional tasks to those required to satisfy the demands of the industrialized world, such as rubber plantations in Southeast Asia.

26. **B**   Social and Gender Structure: 1750–1914

The three Estates had the clergy on top (closest to God?) followed by the nobility, and then everyone else. The first two Estates accounted for roughly 3 percent of the population, but as much as 33 percent of France's wealth. The Third Estate however, paid all the taxes, which led to the meeting of the Estates General and eventually the French Revolution.

27. **D**   Cultural and Intellectual Developments: 1750–1914

It has been argued that the leaders of all revolutions come from the middle (or in some cases upper) classes of society. While the lower classes make up the bulk of the movement, they lack leaders who are educated and have standing in society that helps rally others to their side. Jefferson, Robespierre, Adams, and Marat all fit the description of middle- or upper-class leaders of their revolutions (answer choice **D**). The French leaders did not fight extensively against the troops of Louis XIV as answer choice **A** suggests, and the Americans did not widely execute Loyalists or any other enemies, as the French did in their revolution (answer choice **B**). Neither side was motivated primarily by a chance to get rich (**E**), but the French were also not attempting to establish their own nation that would be self-governing, which was the goal of the Americans (**C**).

28. **A**   Changes in Functions and Structures of States: 1750–1914

Franklin (**C**) and Jefferson (**D**) were key leaders in the American Revolution, whereas Robespierre (**B**) and Marat (**E**) were key figures in the French Revolution. Toussaint L'Overture, however, was a key leader in the Revolution of Haiti.

29. **B**   Cultural and Intellectual Developments: 1914–Present

A complete theocracy is unusual in history. Modern Saudi Arabia offers a good example of why: while the ruling family is secular, and many decisions are not sufficiently in keeping with Islamic law (shari'a) for orthodox Muslims, there is still a clear Islamic moral code that governs the land. Women, for example, are not allowed to drive cars for reasons tied to the Qur'an. The Taliban and Iran's government, answers **A** and **C**, have been ruled much more directly by actual religious leaders. However, Nassar's government in Egypt was not only completely secular but also actually sought to repress Egypt's most vocal Islamic elements. This makes answer choice **B** the correct answer. Secular governments today govern nearly all nations with Islamic majorities.

30.   **C**   Impact of Technology and Demography: 1914–Present

The definitions of "developed" and "developing" are fluid when applied to actual nations. Generally speaking, however, developed nations have low infant mortality, high literacy, and high per capita income relative to developing countries. Developing nations are the opposite: high infant mortality, low literacy, and low per capita income.

31.   **D**   Changes in Functions and Structures of States: 1914–Present

From 1910 until 2000, the government of Mexico had been in control of the PRI, answer choice **D**. In 2000, the National Action Party (PAN) candidate, Vicente Fox, was elected president. The government of Mexico is an important study in postcolonial development, both economically and politically. It has not fallen into the sphere of communism or other radical ideologies that have plagued developing and developed nations alike, nor has it successfully caught up to the industrialized world. One party controlled the government, yet the nation remained a relatively stable democracy for nearly a century.

32.   **A**   Changes in Functions and Structures of States: 1914–Present

The Intifada began in 1987 as an uprising by Palestinians against Israel. What its cause was depends on one's point of view. Some would describe the movement as terrorism, whereas others would describe it as a fight against the occupation of a foreign power. It is not a modernization movement in Iran (choice **B**), although Iran does have a movement (especially among the young) encouraging "modernization." The Turkish government has also prohibited women from following Islamic dress codes at public institutions, such as state-run universities (choice **C**). Parts of Iraq also have large Kurdish populations that might be interested in an independent Kurdish state (choice **D**), although such a movement is not referred to as the Intifada. Egypt has significant Islamic political parties (choice **E**), but they are known by other names.

33.   **A**   Patterns and Impacts of Interaction: 1914–Present

While several of the possible answers are true, only one of them can be tied to the graph. Trade between the United States and China has grown since 1995 (**B**), but the graph does not demonstrate this—only what trade occurred in 1995. Likewise, electronics are an important export for Japan (**C**), but the graph does not break down Japan's trade surplus with the United States by product type. However, Japan is a critical ally of the United States on the Pacific Rim, and the United States does have a significant trade deficit with Japan (as well as other nations). NAFTA (**E**) was not designed to reverse this, as it was a treaty between the United States, Canada, and Mexico. There may be some correlation between government type and the success of a nation's economy (**D**), but regardless, such a generalization is not borne out by the graph. (China's autocratic government is clearly successful in its trade with the United States.)

34.   **E**   Patterns and Impacts of Interaction: 1914–Present

The formation of the twenty-five-member European Union is one of the most important developments of post–Cold War Europe. Most of Western Europe is included, as is much of the former communist Eastern bloc. However, Bulgaria, Romania, and Croatia have not been accepted, eliminating choices **A** and **D**, although Latvia and Poland have. Turkey (**B**) has been lobbying for inclusion, which would mark an important step in European geopolitics, but has not yet been accepted. Turkey is predominantly Muslim, and on the periphery of Europe, but is an important European ally, especially with its proximity to

Southwest Asia (the Mid-East). Russia (**C**) is not a member, but has shown a strong affiliation toward working with the EU.

35.　**B**　Patterns and Impacts of Interaction: 1914–Present
The revolutions of Russia and China were alike in many ways. Obviously, both aimed for a communist takeover of the government, and both occurred in nations that were far more agrarian than industrial (choice **B**). However, only the Chinese revolution could be considered a mass movement (**A**), as Lenin and a small elite core of communists led the Russian movement. Mao and the Chinese communists had spent years cultivating a following among China's peasants, and the movement overthrew a strong ruling party (**C**). The Russian Revolution occurred during the World War I, which was not going well for the future Soviets at the time (choice **D**). In contrast, the Chinese revolution came on the heels of the successful (for China) Second World War. Although the United States did have some involvement in the post-revolutionary Russian civil war, there was no such U.S. incursion into China (choice **E**).

36.　**C**　Social and Gender Structure: 8000 B.C.E.–600 C.E.
Although trade (and therefore merchants) is an important component of any empire, both Roman (**D**) and Han Chinese (**B**) society looked down on merchants. To Confucians, merchants were parasites on society, increasing prices while underpaying producers to derive profits while contributing nothing. Roman society saw trade as beneath the elite, although they often hired "front men" to handle the business for them. Alexander's empire (**E**) covered key trade routes but was too short-lived to expand trade contacts. The Tang dynasty (**A**) held similar views to the Han and is also outside of the time period (founded 618 C.E.). The Gupta/Mauryan Empires (choice **C**) however, were based on cities that were hubs of trade along the Ganges. Merchants were in the third of the four caste tiers and considered an important part of society.

37.　**E**　Social and Gender Structure: 8000 B.C.E.–600 C.E.
Confucianism stressed order in society through a "bottom-up" dynamic. In other words, if people maintained order in society through proper attention to the Five Relationships, there would be little need for a ruler to impose order. The Five Relationships were Ruler and Subject, Father and Son, Husband and Wife, Older and Younger Brother and finally Older and Younger Friend. In the era of Warring States when Confucius was alive, establishing order in society was the goal of many different philosophers and schools of thought. Daoists sought the order of nature, whereas Legalists sought more order imposed by rulers, a "top-down" approach.

38.　**B**　Patterns and Impacts of Interaction: 8000 B.C.E.–600 C.E.
The similarities between Christianity and Judaism are plentiful, as Christianity began as a sect of Judaism. However, Christians believe Jesus was in fact the Messiah or Savior, a belief Jews reject. While dietary restrictions continue to be a part of Orthodox Judaism, there is little sign of such restriction left in Christianity. Judaism generally has respected Jesus as a prophet, but not as divine or a part of God. However, Christians and Jews both abide by the Ten Commandments and view God as monotheistic. Both groups suffered persecution at times at the hands of the Romans.

39.   **D**   The Relationship of Change and Continuity: 8000 B.C.E.–600 C.E.

Most students should be familiar with the schism between the Roman Catholic (**B**) and Eastern Orthodox (**A**) Churches in 1054. However, there were already several other "churches" in existence at that time. The Bishop of Alexandria headed the Coptic Church (**C**), while further to the east most Christians in Persia were Nestorians (**D**). Doctrine and dogma separated the Churches, as did political and personal issues. The nature of Christ as one or two entities, unified or disunified, separated the Nestorians from the rest of Christianity, while the Eastern and Western Churches separated on a series of issues including the use of icons and the proper relationship of the pope or patriarch to the emperor or Holy Roman Emperor. Most of the world's religions have experienced similar splits, as cultural diversification and time erode what always begins as a central message. Only choice **D**, the Lutheran Church, was not a sect of Christianity by 1055.

40.   **E**   Patterns and Impacts of Interaction: 600 C.E.–1450

Certainly silk was a key, perhaps *the* key, commodity traded on the Silk Road (choice **A**). After all, that's its name. However, there is no indication on the map of what was being traded. Likewise, there is no indication of whether the Chinese, pastoralists, or anyone else was able to dominate the trade (choices **B** and **D**). The apparent detours from Dunhuang to Kashgar are due to the Taklamakan Desert, not to frequent bandit attacks as answer choice **C** suggests. The only conclusion that can be drawn from the map is that trade involved cities from China to the Mediterranean Sea, making answer choice **E** the correct answer.

41.   **A**   Patterns and Impacts of Interaction: 600 C.E.–1450

One of the most frequent depictions of Muslims by non-Muslims in this period was that they were much "cleaner" than other people. In fact, this was due to the frequent bathing, at least of the arms and head, which faithful Muslims performed before daily prayers. As important as cleanliness was, however, it was not one of the Five Pillars, making answer choice **A** the correct answer. All of the other options make up four of the Five Pillars of Islam, with alms for the poor absent from the list. This question involves patterns of interaction, because Islam views itself as a continuation of Judaism and Christianity. (The founder of both Judaism and Islam was Abraham, whose sons Isaac and Ishmael were the ancestors of the Jews and Muslims, respectively.) Islam also borrowed from the local Arabic beliefs when they made Mecca a place of worship. While the Prophet did receive the Qur'an in the hills near the city, it had previously been a place of pilgrimage for Arabs all across the peninsula—a tradition that continued under Islam.

42.   **A**   Impact of Technology and Demography: 600 C.E.–1450

The dwellings of pastoral nomads are generally made to be movable, as the herds (of camels, horses, or buffalo) are regularly on the move. Native Americans on the Plains also followed the herds, but they were more pastoral than nomadic. Both groups therefore made their dwellings to be easily transportable. Additionally, both yurts and teepees were made of wooden supports covered by animal hides. Answer choice **A** is the correct answer. While some yurts could indicate status, teepees did not indicate this (on the basis of size [choice **C**]) and they were not constructed in any particular direction (choice **B**). Because these dwellings were not permanent, they cannot be excavated by archeologists (choice **D**). Openings at the top were for ventilation, with any ceremonial function being only secondary (choice **E**).

43. **C** Cultural and Intellectual Developments: 600 C.E.–1450

The quote in the question suggests both diffusion from east to west and navigational development (choice **C**). This pattern rules out any diffusion from west to east (choice **D**), as well as the development of triangular sails on the Indian Ocean (choice **E**). While Muslim mathematics was advanced, there is no suggestion of diffusion in answer choice **B**. The same holds true for the fictional development of the astrolabe by Venetians (choice **A**), which dates back possibly as far as ancient Greece.

44. **A** Changes in Functions and Structures of States: 600 C.E.–1450

Many conquered people made up part of the Aztec Empire, and the Aztecs extracted heavy tribute from them, sometimes even using them for human sacrifices. While Aztec kings often taxed farmers on land within the empire (**B**), and also pressed local villagers into serving the empire in the army (**C**), these were not reasons for Native American support of Cortes. While the natives found horses strange, they were not motivated by a fear of the animals to assist Cortez (**E**), and the Native American culture did not require assistance be granted to strangers (**D**).

45. **E** Patterns and Impacts of Interaction: 600 C.E.–1450

Marco Polo was a young Italian merchant who journeyed with his father and uncle across Eurasia to China. During the reign of Kublai Khan, Polo found work in the Great Khan's court. More importantly perhaps, upon his return, Polo had his account of his years of wandering around Eurasia written down. (Polo himself was illiterate and so employed someone to write his memoirs for him. For this reason, some historians have doubts about the validity of the manuscript and have speculated that Polo did not reach China at all.) Salah al-Din, choice **A**, in contrast, is noted for his opposition to the Christian Crusaders and his capture of Jerusalem in 1187, not for his travels. Moses Maimonides, choice **C**, was a famed Jewish scholar in medieval Muslim Spain (1135–1204). Omar Khay'yam, choice **D**, was a Muslim poet best known for his poem "The Rubaiyat" (1120). However, the remaining two choices did make lengthy journeys like Polo. Mansa Musa, choice **B**, was a king of Mali who made a pilgrimage to Mecca in 1324. Unlike Polo, however, the king had great wealth and status and was traveling mostly through "Dar al-Islam," or Islamic lands. Ibn Battuta also traveled through Islamic lands at times, but made a trip of an estimated 73,000 miles, over 29 years, through many nations. He also wrote extensively of his journeys, making him the correct answer.

46. **B** Patterns and Impacts of Interaction: 600 C.E.–1450

The Vikings are remembered for their fierce attacks on medieval monasteries and towns, in part permitted by the shallow hulls (bottoms) of their boats (**B**). These hulls allowed the Vikings to sail down the Seine and other rivers of modern France and Russia for attack or trade, including an 861 attack on Paris. Because the boats had masts, they could not be turned over for shelters on shore, eliminating answer choice **D**. They also did not have areas for storage "below deck" of any significance (**C**). While they were seaworthy enough to have reached Iceland, Greenland, and beyond, the Vikings are not known to have ventured down the African coast (**E**). Viking writing was in the form of runes (symbols), generally only for ritual and not derived from Greek (**B**). The Vikings were early settlers of modern Russia, however, whose alphabet (Cyrillic) is based on Greek.

47.   **C**   Impact of Technology and Demography: 600 C.E.–1450

The migrations of the Bantu from the Niger River region throughout much of the rest of sub-Saharan Africa have many similarities to the migrations of the Germanic peoples into Europe. Both groups displaced some local inhabitants and diffused their cultures within the regions they entered (**C**). The Bantu, however, were in no way connected to the Roman demise (**A**), having begun their movement centuries before Rome was founded. There is evidence that the Bantu had iron technology as the Germanic tribes certainly did, and iron would have been far superior to bronze for weapons (**D**). Neither group was reliant upon wheat or fishing, although wheat would not have been unknown to the Germanic peoples (**E**).

48.   **E**   Changes in Functions and Structures of States: 600 C.E.–1450

Assuming the Renaissance spans 1300–1600, the Schism of the Church (1054) is incorrect (**D**). Likewise, Constantinople's fall, choice **A**, in 1453 and the independence movement of the Netherlands, choice **B**, which concluded in 1609, are too late. The Mongol invasions (**C**) were primarily an East European and Russian concern, while the Renaissance was a movement in Western Europe. The Hundred Years' War however, choice **E**, from 1337 to 1453, not only took place in the beginning of the Renaissance but also helped to define the relationship between England and France, which had been unclear since William of Normandy (a vassal to the king of France) had become king of England in 1066. The war permanently separated the identities of Frenchmen and Englishmen.

49.   **D**   Patterns and Impacts of Interaction: 600 C.E.–1450

The archipelago of Southeast Asia has long attracted visitors for a variety of reasons. Winds made it easy to get to (**E**), and products, such as spice (**C**), made it worthwhile. The geography enabled many groups to control trade in the area for a time (**B**). Thus, wave upon wave of peoples have descended on these islands. Indian influence can still be felt, for example, in the Hinduism on Bali. Yet Indonesia is the largest Muslim nation in the world (by population) thanks to the Arab merchants of the Indian Ocean. The Chinese regularly moored there to trade and wait for the right winds to take them into the Indian Ocean (**A**). And the Dutch and Portuguese each tried to control the Strait of Malacca, so as to regulate (and charge fees on) the lucrative trade. For this reason, the Dutch set up shop in Batavia, modern day Djakarta. The only reason listed that was not a reason why the islands held such a vast array of cultural elements is choice **D**. Local rulers are not known to have offered refuge to an particular group.

50.   **A**   Social and Gender Structure: 1450–1750

The encomienda system differed from feudalism in one key way: Feudal kings owned their land as a right of birth, and were sovereign unless they were vassals to greater kings. The landowners of encomiendas, however, were given their lands by grants from the king of Spain and answered to the viceroy or the "local" Spanish governor. These landowners therefore could not "knight" former colleagues. The encomienda system was eventually abolished in 1542, in part because of the protests of Bartolome De Las Casas, a Spanish monk and missionary to New Spain. Las Casas objected quite effectively to the treatment of the natives. However, the natives who worked the encomiendas were considered a part of the "land grant" in the way the medieval serfs, while not slaves per se, were part of the land in the feudal system, and could be bought and sold with it, making choice **A** the correct answer.

51. **C** Social and Gender Structure: 1450–1750
While most cultures subjugated women to men's interests, there have been many note-worthy exceptions to the rule. The list of women in the question represents only five of the many who overcame expectations and rose to the ultimate position of power in their land. Elizabeth I, choice **A**, ruled England from 1558 to 1603. Likewise, Marie-Therese of Austria, choice **B**, was Queen of the Austrian-Hungarian Empire from 1745 to 1780. Isabella of Castile, choice **D**, united her nation with Aragon through her marriage to Ferdinand and reigned from 1469 to 1504. Queen Nzinga, choice **E**, of the Matamba (modern day Angola) led her people in resistance to Portuguese slavers, during her reign c.1623 to 1663. And Empress Dowager Cixi reigned over the Qing dynasty from 1881 until 1908. However her rule is almost a century after the time period given in the question, making choice **C** the correct answer.

52. **B** Changes in Functions and Structures of States: 1450–1750
A powerful individual—the Ottoman Sultan, and the Safavid Persian Shah—ruled each empire, and while each kingdom was responsive to Islamic scholars (the *ulama*), the scholars were not the rulers. The expanse of the Ottoman Empire at its height stretched from Mesopotamia to north of the Black Sea, and from the Balkans across North Africa. The Safavid Empire included modern Iran and some surrounding areas. Both empires were predominantly land based, although the Ottoman fleet prevented the Europeans from doing much on the Mediterranean for many years. The division between the empires regarding Islam, however, is the major distinguishing feature. The Ottomans were Sunni Muslims and the Safavids were Shi'ite. These divisions can be seen today in the religious divisions of nations in the Middle East, such as Iraq.

53. **B** The Relationship of Change and Continuity: 1450–1750
The era of European expansion brought many changes to Africa, but slavery was not one of them, as answer choice **E** suggests. Slavery had existed in Africa for centuries, though never in the volume the Europeans would demand. Gold also left Africa for Europe, but not in enough quantity to destabilize the European economy (choice **D**). While germs probably passed between business partners, Europe did not suffer any waves of sickness as a result of contact with Africa (choice **C**) nor did Africans boycott their old Muslim merchant friends (choice **A**). The patterns of trade, however, choice **B**, did begin to change. As the Europeans appeared on the Atlantic coast, nations such as Benin and Ibo became more powerful, whereas cities on the trans-Saharan route, like Timbuktu, began to fade.

54. **E** Cultural and Intellectual Developments: 1450–1750
Martin Luther had many objections to Church teaching—ninety-five of them, in fact, which he famously wrote out and nailed to the door of the Wittenberg church in Germany. While he felt that the Bible and mass should be in the local language, choice **A**, that objection is not reflected in the quote. He also objected to the wealth of some clergymen, choice **D**, and to the notion of salvation being gained through anything but faith in God, choice **C**, but neither of these objections is reflected by the quote. Instead, the quote refers to the sale of indulgences, or forgiveness of sins in return for donations to the Church, choice **E**, which sellers like Tetzel said would limit a soul's time in purgatory. While this was not charging for performing rites, choice **B**, Luther found it abhorrent on several fronts, and it is that sentiment that is reflected in the quote.

55.   **A**   Changes in Functions and Structures of States: 1450–1750

While the Mughal Empire was certainly part of the Indian Ocean trade, its economy was not revived by the commerce (choice **B**). France was more focused on colonizing North America and improving its domestic economy. Neither made significant improvements in the status of women or slaves, as choice **C** indicates, and neither created syncretic religions, choice **D**, as Aurangazeb's grandfather, Akbar, had tried to do. Instead, both were religiously intolerant, choice **A**. The Mughal Emperor persecuted Hindus, and the French monarch persecuted Protestant Huguenots. Yet despite these religious intolerances, each expanded the borders of his realm through conquest.

56.   **C**   Patterns and Impacts of Interaction: 1450–1750

Here are the battles listed in chronological order: Manzikert (1071), in which the Muslims defeated the Byzantines; Agincourt (1415), a defeat of the French by the English in the Hundred Years' War; the defeat of the Aztecs and Montezuma from 1519 to 1522; the Battle of Diu (1509), a naval victory for Portugal over the Muslims of the Indian Ocean; Lepanto (1571), a major naval battle between Christian and Muslim forces that eliminated the Ottomans as a major force in the Mediterranean; the defeat of the Spanish Armada by the English (1588), ending its reign of oceanic supremacy; Napoleon's defeat on the Mediterranean at the Battle of the Nile (1798); and Napoleon's defeat on land at Waterloo (1815). Using the time period in the question, 1450 to 1750, choices **B**, **D**, and **E** can be eliminated. Of the remaining two options, only choice **C** involves two naval engagements during the appropriate time period.

57.   **E**   Patterns and Impacts of Interaction: 1450–1750

The Canton System, as it was called, was instituted by the Qing dynasty c. 1759, and lasted until roughly 1842, the end of the first Opium War. During this time, European merchants were only allowed to do business with the Chinese in the city of Guangzhou, also know as Canton. Chinese customs officials kept an eye on the trade and collected tribute from the Europeans in return for the right to trade with "the Middle Kingdom."

58.   **E**   Patterns and Impacts of Interaction: 1750–1914

Any statement about European colonization in the Americas is likely to be a generalization. However, the differences between the colonizing techniques of the English and French can be summarized in the following way: the French sent both Catholics and Protestants (the Huguenots), as did the English, who were glad to be rid of the Puritans who had caused so much trouble in England, so choice **A** is incorrect. Generally, the French profited the most from the sugar of Haiti and the furs of North America and sent comparatively few colonists to the New World, but by no means did they only send male colonists (choice **C**), nor were they most interested in establishing colonies, as choice **B** indicates. Since England had many other colonies, including growing interests in India and China, the lack of revenue from the American colonies did not pose that big of a problem for the crown, as choice **D** states. That leaves choice **E**, and although the French did not always get along perfectly with the natives, their relations were for the most part peaceful, whereas the English colonists' relations with the natives were generally hostile. Choice **E** is the correct answer.

59.   **A**   Changes in Functions and Structures of States: 1750–1914

Through his efforts, Simon Bolivar won independence for Bolivia, Columbia, Panama, Ecuador, Peru, and Venezuela. At the time, these were not all separate nations, but they all owed their independence from Spain to "El Liberator." L'Overture, choice **B**, was only involved in the revolution in Haiti, while Padre Hidalgo, choice **D**, was a figure from the Mexican Revolution. Las Casas, choice **C**, was not a revolutionary but instead a Spanish missionary who championed the rights of the native peoples of New Spain. Oddly enough, the figure with the most responsibility for independence movements in the New World (besides Bolivar) might have been Napoleon, choice **E**. His conquests in Europe, including Spain, weakened European control over colonies such as Mexico and Haiti and gave their independence movements a head start.

60.   **A**   Impact of Technology and Demography: 1750–1914

Manifest Destiny has been called both an ideal and a justification. It refers to the expansion of the United States toward the Pacific, especially in the 1800s. Whether it was the duty of white Americans to spread their political and spiritual dreams to the less fortunate inhabitants of the West (i.e., Native Americans and Mexicans) or simply an excuse to annex land depends largely on one's point of view. The other four statements are fictional, although they involve topics relevant to America during this century: the war with Mexico (**D**), a spiritual revival (**E**), growing global trade (**C**), and the ultimate fate of America's remaining native population (**B**).

61.   **E**   Patterns and Impacts of Interaction: 1750–1914

Both the Boxer Rebellion of China and the Indian National Congress were intent on removing foreigners from their nation (or at least from control of their nation). Western military forces eventually put down the Boxer Rebellion, but India became independent (albeit in 1948) thanks to the leadership of Mohandas Gandhi, Jawaharlal Nehru, Muhammad Ali Jinnah, and others. In neither case was a monarchy the goal, although a native government certainly was.

62.   **A**   Patterns and Impacts of Interaction: 1750–1914

Some historians have called the Seven Years' War (1756–1763) the first truly "world" war because it was fought in India, Europe, and North America (where it is commonly called the French and Indian War). The two primary combatants were the British and the French. The Dutch were not principally involved in the fighting, although it was Dutch settlers (called "Boers") in South Africa who stubbornly resisted the British in the Boer War (1899–1902), fought solely in Africa (eliminating choice **B**). Neither involved religion or benefited the Dutch, choice **E** and **C** respectively. The Boers ultimately lost, as did the motherland, by extension. Both wars were over colonial possessions, and in some aspects (North America being one) they did involve indigenous peoples, but the Boers were themselves European colonizers, not natives to South Africa, eliminating choice **D**.

63.   **D**   Patterns and Impacts of Interaction: 1750–1914

Beginning under President Taft in the early years of the twentieth century, the United States began to intervene in the internal affairs of several nations in Latin America. The motive for these interventions was to safeguard the investments of American corporations in these nations. Ultimately, the policy was not terribly successful at preventing major political disruptions in Mexico, Nicaragua, and other nations. The United States did buy Alaska in 1867 and the Gadsden Purchase was made in 1853, as indicated in choice **C**, but these were not part of the Dollar Diplomacy approach. Similarly, the strategy was not an attempt to increase exports and high tariffs to improve trade (choice **E**), an effort to keep the dollar tied to the gold standard (choice **A**), or a way to improve goodwill among foreign nations (choice **B**).

64. **D**   Patterns and Impacts of Interaction: 1750–1914
There are two keys to answering this question: The first is not to waste time doing math unless you have to. If all the other answers seem wrong, you might want to try some math to see if the answer about ratios is true. The better option is to choose the right answer based on knowledge of the causes of World War I, not the graph per se. Austria-Hungary declared war on Serbia (which isn't on the graph). Those actions prompted Russia to declare war in Serbia's defense. This brought Germany into the war as Austria's ally. The United States didn't enter the war until 1917, which helps explain why so few Americans (relatively speaking) were killed.

65. **C**   The Relationship of Change and Continuity: 1914–Present
All of the answers represent significant challenges to modern sub-Saharan African nations, except choice **C**. Furthermore, many of these problems can be traced back to the colonial era and beyond. For example, most financiers and bureaucrats under the European colonial administrations were Europeans, not natives of the country under colonial rule. When colonialism ended, the political and economically experienced figures left the newly independent Africans to fend for themselves. In addition, African history before colonialism gave little hint of interest to democracy or progressive political ideals, preferring instead the "strong man" or tribal chief/council figures that ran the nations as their own personal fiefs. This lack of experienced leadership (and in some cases, outright corruption) has led to the various problems that continue to plague modern sub-Saharan Africa today.

66. **C**   Social and Gender Structure: 1914–Present
Women in many nations, including the Unites States, received the right to vote in the years that followed the First World War. The League of Nations, however, was not responsible, as choice **A** indicates. Additionally, sati was far from common in India and had been outlawed for some time, eliminating choice **B**. Given the number of women in the Muslim world, a change in their rights would be tremendous, but the Muslim world is not homogeneous. Women in Turkey have many freedoms women in Saudi Arabia can only dream of, yet these are both Muslim nations. Further, according to *shari'a* (Islamic law) a woman is allowed to divorce, eliminating choice **D**. Finally, the Catholic Church has not ordained any women as priests, and seems unlikely to in the near future, which eliminates choice **E**.

67. **D**   Cultural and Intellectual Developments: 1914–Present
Mohandas Gandhi and Muhammad Ali Jinnah were both key figures working for the independence of India from Britain. Jinnah was not as devoted to nonviolence (choice **B**) as Gandhi was, and he wanted the country partitioned so that Muslims would be in the majority in the "Pakistans." Gandhi opposed this plan. Gandhi was from the Gujarat region of India, but Ali Jinnah was not, and even though the region has a large Muslim minority, Gandhi himself was a Hindu. Each man is a hero in his country today, not just in Pakistan.

68. E   Social and Gender Structure: 1914–Present

The first thing to notice about this question is that four of the options (all wrong) are absolutes. That is, the four that claim to apply to "all" or invoke "never" can be suspected of being wrong right away, because it only takes one exception to make the statement false. For example, many revolutions (e.g., the Chinese and Russian) gave more rights to women—but not all, as was the case in Iran. Some religions may originate with the upper class, but most are driven by the lower (with the most to gain) and the middle classes. Many revolutions are about economics, but Iran's (again) was about culture and religion. If a revolution does not involve the economy of the country, it's likely not going to include Marxism either. Again, be wary of "absolutes." Choice **E** is the correct answer.

69. C   Impact of Technology and Demography: 1914–Present

The motto of many Holocaust survivors in Nazi Germany was "Never again" (choice **D**). Sadly, genocide has been no stranger in the last century. The Khmer Rouge of Cambodia killed roughly one-third of its own people while trying to create a perfect communist state (choice **A**). Stalin's Soviet Union saw the exile of thousands to the gulags of Siberia and starvation of thousands more in the Ukraine (choice **B**). In Rwanda, violence between Hutus and Tutsis led to the deaths of thousands (choice **E**). There were also many deaths during the civil wars in Nicaragua. But not all deaths are genocidal. In Nicaragua, there was no attempt made to exterminate a group of people on the basis of some characteristic in an organized manner. Thus, while tragic, the Nicaraguan option is still not an example of genocide.

70. A   Cultural and Intellectual Developments: 1914–Present

The key to answering this question is to understand that the quote focuses on the power of individuals and highlights the effects of individuals on globalization as being something new. The latter criterion rules out dictators, as they aren't new arrivals to the globalization debate. The stipulation for individuals rules out the media, nation-states, and major economic or religious institutions. What are left are two individuals who have had a tremendous impact on their countries. Aung San Su Kyi, democracy advocate from Myanmar, has spent much of the last decade in prison or under house arrest. Yet she won the Nobel Peace Prize in 1991. Bin Laden's isolation is self-imposed, hiding from those governments and others seeking to bring him to justice for his role in terrorist activity. Yet his role is alleged to be that of a mastermind of terrorism worldwide. Videos he releases periodically immediately appear on CNN and other media outlets. This is the globalization the quote is referring to, and answer **A** is the correct choice.

SECTION II: FREE-RESPONSE EXPLANATIONS

Question 1: Document Based Question

Sample DBQ Essay

Ancient Greek civilization and ancient Chinese civilization both made a lasting impression on the history of mankind. Each civilization's views of the individual, however, were very different in political, religious, and daily life. In religious terms, the Chinese saw people as part of a bigger, grand plan; the Greeks believed that each man was his own entity. In political affairs, the Greeks pioneered democracy, valuing each citizen's contribution; the Chinese, in contrast, preferred everyone loyally serve the emperor. In daily life, Greek civilization recognized each individual as distinct; in China, each man was like one strand in a very large web. In short, the Greeks and Chinese views of the individual in society were very different on the spiritual, governmental, and social levels.

In religious terms, the Greeks saw themselves as actors upon the cosmic stage. They were often involved in the myths of their gods, and might even have individual relationships with the deities. The Greeks even fashioned their gods to look like themselves, as Document 1 points out. This stands in stark contrast to the three main Chinese religions/philosophies—Confucianism, Taoism, and Buddhism. To the Chinese, each individual was part of something beyond himself. Each man was part of the past and the future, part yin and part yang. All things were connected, as suggested by Document 2. Of these three religions, Buddhism is the youngest, introduced hundreds of years after Taoism and Confucianism had become popular in China. A valuable document not present would be from an Indian Buddhist in China, at a time before Buddhism was popular. As an outsider, this observer could give us an objective view of Buddhism (and Greek religion too, if he was a traveler) which would insure a reliable point of reference. The Indian would no doubt agree that Chinese religions saw individuals as parts of a whole, not as individuals apart from the whole.

On the political front, the Greeks are famous for their introduction of the democratic form of government. Unlike most other forms of government, democracy required all citizens to be involved in the political process and responsible for their civic duties. In turn, all citizens could have a say in the laws that governed the land: "a commonwealth without monarchy," as Document 2 calls it. Unfortunately, Document 2 is not a terribly reliable document. The author, Plutarch, was writing well after the age of the Greeks, under the rule of the Roman Empire. Plutarch's writings are legendary for their moral tone, and Theseus is considered a "folkloric" figure. It's very possible that Plutarch was trying to give a "lesson" to his readers throughout the empire about how wonderful the current system of government was. This makes the document suspect, which is why Document 8 is crucial. Document 8 states that the preferred Greek fighting style (the phalanx) required lots of men to work as one. These men wouldn't risk their lives unless they could be rewarded with some say in government. Since "it placed the noble and the ordinary citizen on an equality in the field," the phalanx helped shape the democratic ideal in Greece.

China, meanwhile, had no such inclination. The emperor was a father figure and his subjects were children. They had no rights as we would see it, nor input in the government. The subjects were simply expected to do as they were told, as implied in Document 6. As with Document 2, Document 6 may not be completely reliable as a reflection of Chinese government since it was written by a Legalist and only gives that school's view of the people. The view of Confucians or Taoists might be more generous to the average person in China. However, while the document should be viewed with caution, it is further evidence that the average citizen in China held little to no political power.

Finally, as with religious and political life, there are some clear differences between these two cultures with regard to daily life. Most Greek and Chinese citizens were farmers, seldom traveling far from home, and valuing their faiths and families. They received little formal schooling and were largely unconcerned with the ways of the government. But the Greek society was more inclined to overlook issues of social difference. This may seem odd for a people who practiced slavery, but Document 4 implies that any citizen, regardless of their social class, could participate in government. Like the phalanx, the town meeting could be a place where the upper and lower classes rubbed elbows (figuratively, at least).

In the strict hierarchy of China, this would not have been as likely. The Five Relationships of Confucianism stress that there is a superior and inferior in all pairings (e.g., Father/Son, Husband/Wife). This point is repeated in Document 5, in which Confucius himself divides people into the "superiors" and "inferiors," or those who must bend, and those who do the bending. We can be confident that this document gives an accurate portrayal of Chinese society for two reasons. First, it comes from Confucius himself, or at least the closest thing we have to a quote, so no one is interpreting it for us. Second, Confucianism became the dominant philosophy in China in the second century B.C.E. and in many ways is still a part of Chinese culture today. Thus, this document is a very reliable source when it spells out the hierarchy of Chinese society.

Even in death, the Chinese were part of a pecking order, with ancestors literally being worshiped, as Document 3 points out. Arguably, no one in ancient China could have been equal to anyone else, whereas in Greece, everyone was equal to everyone else. However, none of these documents specifically refer to women or their roles in government, religion, or society. If we had the testimony, perhaps in a diary, of an ancient Greek or Chinese woman, we might see that their societies were even more different. Other documents and traditions from the time tell us that both Chinese and Greek women had no rights. But they would at least be able to give us another lens through which to see these issues.

In conclusion, the Greeks and Chinese views of the individual in society were very different on the spiritual, governmental, and social levels. In religious terms, the Chinese saw people as part of a great plan, whereas to the Greeks each man was his own entity. In political affairs, the Greeks pioneered democracy, valuing each citizen's contribution. The Chinese, in contrast, preferred that everyone loyally serve the emperor. Even in daily life, the Greek civilization recognized each individual as distinct, whereas in China each man was like one strand in a web. Both worldviews are still a part of the cultures of each society today.

DBQ Essay Discussion

The DBQ is scored on a 9-point scale along the following guidelines:

1. Provides an acceptable thesis—1 point
2. Uses all or all but one of the documents—1 point
3. Shows an understanding of all or all but one of the cited documents—1 point
4. Supports thesis with evidence from the documents—1 point
5. Analyzes point of view in at least two documents—1 point
6. Addresses question by grouping documents in a certain way, depending on the question—1 point
7. Identifies one type of additional document—1 point.

To earn the remaining two points, the essay must expand beyond these "basic" points, including analyzing the point of view of all documents, bringing in many additional documents and outside information, and showing especially insightful analysis. The sample essay provided is an example of a high-scoring essay that accomplishes many of these things. Let's look at it in depth.

The first step to writing an answer to an AP World History document-based question is to realize that there is no one right answer. In the question above, for example, a student could argue that China and Greece were different because of their religions, politics, social values, military styles, philosophies (perhaps as a result of geography), etc. Another student might argue that the two societies were very similar. Although the question requires the student to discuss the individual's role and the roles people played in society (ruler, soldier, father) the specifics of the essay are up to each student's creativity and knowledge base. Likewise, other points may be included beyond what is required, especially if those points help shed a clearer light on where the documents are from, who wrote them, or any other contextual information. In other words, there are a lot of good ways to write an AP World History document-based question. There are, however, some general points that should be represented in each of them.

The Thesis Statement: The first goal of every student should be to draft an introductory paragraph with a comprehensive and analytical thesis.

Let's look at the thesis statement from the sample essay.

Thesis Statement:
Ancient Greek civilization and ancient Chinese civilization both made a lasting impression on the history of mankind. Each civilization's views of the individual, however, were very different in political, religious, and daily life. In religious terms, the Chinese saw people as part of a bigger, grand plan; the Greeks believed that each man was his own entity. In political affairs, the Greeks pioneered democracy, valuing each citizen's contribution; the Chinese, in contrast, preferred that everyone loyally serve the emperor. In daily life, Greek civilization recognized each individual as distinct; in China, each person was like one strand in a very large web. In short, <u>the Greeks and Chinese views of the individual in society were very different on the spiritual, governmental, and social levels.</u>

The thesis statement has been underlined. This introductory paragraph tells the reader what the argument is (the views of the Greeks and Chinese were different) and gives a glimpse of the direction the rest of the essay will go. Each of the three key points (spiritual, governmental, and social) will become the topic of one of the body paragraphs.

Of course, in order to formulate a thesis to this question, you'd have to know what your response was going to be. For that, you first need to sort the documents into groups depending on how you plan to use them. For example, Documents 1 and 7 involve views of religion. Documents 2, 6, and 8 involve views of government. Social issues are discussed in Documents 3, 4, and 5. There are other groupings possible, but for this sample essay we'll use these. Once the groupings are identified, along with their topics, you can create a thesis and an introductory paragraph. Now let's look at the body paragraphs.

The Supporting (Body) Paragraphs: The body paragraphs will each deal with one of the three sets of documents that we grouped above. As an example, let's look at the social category (Documents 3, 4, and 5). What can we say about the differences between Greece and China based on these documents? Many students try to summarize each document, writing a paragraph like this:

> **Supporting Paragraph:**
> *There were also social differences between Greece and China. Document 4 says that class equality in government also carried over to Greek society. But Document 3 says that Chinese citizens went to worship the graves of the ancestors. Document 5 says superiors outranked inferiors in society.*

This is a common error. In this paragraph the student has simply summarized the documents without applying them to the thesis, and therefore to the question asked. This doesn't move the argument forward. Imagine a lawyer in a trial: He or she doesn't just show the evidence, saying only, "This is a gun and this is bag of money." He or she states an argument ("the defendant had every reason to commit this crime") and backs it up with evidence ("by assaulting the bank guard, the defendant was able to take this bag of cash."). Your arguments, your points, and your ideas are most important in a DBQ. However, you must show how the documents support what you are saying. A better way to handle supporting paragraphs would be like this:

> **Supporting Paragraph:**
> *As with religious and political life, there are some clear differences between these two cultures with regard to daily life. Most Greek and Chinese citizens were farmers, seldom traveling far from home, and valuing their faiths and families. They received little formal schooling and were largely unconcerned with the ways of the government. But the Greek society was more inclined to overlook issues of social difference. This may seem odd for a people who practiced slavery, but Document 4 implies that any citizen, regardless of their social class, could participate in government. Like the phalanx, the town meeting could be a place where the upper and lower classes rubbed elbows (figuratively, at least). In the strict hierarchy of China, this would not have been as likely. The Five Relationships of Confucianism stress that there is a superior and inferior in all pairings (e.g., Father/Son, Husband/Wife). This point is repeated in Document 5, in which Confucius himself divides people into the "superiors" and "inferiors," or those who must bend, and those who do the bending.*

This paragraph uses the documents to support the thesis. Be sure to write an essay in which the documents support your point, not one in which you try to support the documents. If you build each body paragraph like this one you will be in good shape.

The two most important parts of a DBQ essay are the thesis paragraph and the supporting (body) paragraphs. However, there are two remaining sections that will earn you the maximum number of points on the DBQ: Point of View (POV) statements and the Additional Documents statements.

Point of View Statements: An additional way you need to support your thesis is by evaluating the reliability of at least three of the documents. Some documents are less reliable than others because the author is either knowingly or unknowingly misleading the reader. This is called analyzing the document's point of view (POV). For example, if a politician were to give a speech during a campaign promising programs for a special interest group, he might be saying exactly what he feels. It's also possible, however, that he feels the need to say whatever is necessary to get elected, or to not get "booed" off the stage. If we had access to his diary, we could be very confident that it contained his true feelings. Many other issues affect reliability besides the audience. Consider what you know about the author—Was he or she part of some political or religious group? What time period did the author live in? Could that have affected their ability to be objective?

Consider the following example:

POV example:

Unfortunately, this is not a terribly reliable document. The author, Plutarch, was writing well after the age of the Greeks, under the rule of the Roman Empire. Plutarch's writings are legendary for their moral tone, and Theseus is considered a "folkloric" figure. It's very possible that Plutarch was trying to give a "lesson" to his readers on an empire, about how great democracy was. This makes the document suspect...

A paragraph similar to this one is needed to earn the maximum amount of points on the DBQ.

Additional Documents Statement: A final component of an AP World History DBQ is the "additional documents" statement. In this case, the student must act like a historian and consider what type of information NOT provided by the documents would help to answer the question. Since you get to create it yourself, you may as well have it add to your point. Consider if there are voices not being heard, such as that of women or men, slaves, rulers, nobles, or colonists. Also, consider if there are types of information that would help, such as demographics or election returns. If there were a chart that accompanied these documents, what might it show? Here's an example:

Additional Documents example:

A valuable document not present would be from an Indian Buddhist in China, at a time before Buddhism was popular. As an outsider, this observer could give us an objective view of Buddhism (and Greek religion too, if he was a traveler) which would insure us a reliable point of reference. The Indian would no doubt agree that Chinese religions saw individuals as parts of a whole, not as individuals apart from the whole.

A good place to put additional documents is in paragraphs where you have the fewest documents from the DBQ. Be careful, however, not to ask for documents that are in some way already present. In this DBQ, it would be unacceptable to say, "There ought to be a document from a Chinese philosopher speaking about Chinese government." That document already exists (Document 6) and would therefore not earn you any more points.

Some final notes are worthy of mention. Read each document carefully to ensure you know what each one means. Double check to make sure that you have used all the documents, if possible. You can earn a point on the rubric for using "all but one" of the documents, which means you can eliminate one from your analysis if you don't understand it, or if it seems like it doesn't fit with any of your groupings. Also, try to include more than one additional document and analyze the reliability of more than half of the documents, if you have time. Both of these elements will earn you extra points from the rubric. If you do not have time for these "extras" don't worry. Focus on getting the basic points, or you won't be able to earn expanded points at all.

Question 2: Change over Time

Sample Essay Response

The impact of colonialism on India has been dramatic. Modern India has been shaped politically by its past role as a British colony. This role has also affected India's current economic status in the world, for better and worse. Finally, British colonial culture had a large impact on Indian culture, and the colonial government's footprints are still quite visible today. In short, colonialism changed India tremendously politically, economically, and culturally between 1750 and today.

The first British sailors to establish themselves in India were representatives of the British East India Company. They received permission to establish a base in 1619 and founded Madras in 1639. India at this time was under the control of the Muslim Mughal dynasty. Indian Hindu culture had been mixed to varying degrees with the Muslim and Turkish cultures of the Mughals. India was a key player in the Indian Ocean trade and manufactured the most coveted cotton textiles in the world. But by 1750, India had begun to decline. The Mughal emperor Aurangzeb had died in 1707 and left an overextended empire governed by local rulers. The East India Company, which had been increasing its strength over the years, increased its stature by securing those areas that were part of its supply of goods. While they didn't have many British troops, the company made up for this by hiring and training Indian soldiers, called sepoys. *By 1856, the East India Company controlled a vast stretch of India. In 1857, however, a revolt broke out among the sepoys. While this revolt was soon put down, the British government took over, naming a viceroy to oversee the region. This began the long process of diffusing British culture into India. Schools were built, along with railroads and hospitals. Indians became familiar with the British political tradition of democracy and nationalism. By the time of the First World War, Indians were agitating for independence. The First and Second World Wars, along with British reluctance, delayed India's independence until 1948. After the Second World War, however, Britain simply didn't have the means to keep India under its control. When it achieved independence, India became a democracy in the tradition set by the British. Today, India is the largest democracy in the world. It has survived the assassination of leaders and its division into Pakistan and Bangladesh, which was completed in 1948. One reason Western nations have sided with India in its disputes with Pakistan is because India has such a stable, representative government.*

India has also changed economically. In 1750, India was one of the world's leading manufacturing centers. Indian textiles, especially cotton, were prized from Beijing to Jenne. With the increasing control of the British East India Company and the British government, however, the Indian economy began to de-industrialize. By the time of the Sepoy Revolt in 1857, India's economy had become largely dedicated to producing raw cotton, which was exported to mills in Manchester and Leeds. The relationship grew even closer once the American Civil War (1860–1865) took the American cotton supply out of British hands. India has not yet regained its status as a manufacturing power, but since its independence in 1948 it has grown as a force in the global economy. Today, one of India's main exports is computer software. India can produce this cutting-edge technology because it has many educated citizens, most of whom speak English. In fact, many American companies like General Electric now have customer service call centers in India. These changes are the result of both regional and global factors. Since independence, Indians have reasserted their economic might along with their political freedom. When Indians have controlled their own destiny, they have been quite successful.

Finally, India has changed culturally. In 1750, Indian women occasionally committed traditional ritual suicide, sati, *(if they didn't have children) at their husband's funerals. These Hindu women believed that they would be spiritually rewarded for this act of devotion and that it was a woman's duty to be loyal to her husband, even in death. The influence of the British began to change all this. The English language was introduced. Since it was the new language of government, many Indians learned to speak it. The British worked to outlaw sati, as they built infrastructure including telegraph lines to bring India into the world economy. By 1857, the growing number of Indians educated by the British was beginning to understand concepts like nationalism and democracy. The education of Mohandas Gandhi, for example, taught him that everyone should be equal, regardless of caste. By the time India became independent, it was ready to join the "global village" as both a contributor and a receiver of culture. India today produces hundreds of movies each year in "Bollywood" and many are in English. There are over twenty languages spoken in India, but many people speak English as a first or second language, thanks to the British. Likewise, cricket, a popular game in Britain, is also very popular in India today.*

In short, colonialism changed India tremendously between 1750 and today, in political, economic, and cultural ways. Modern India has been shaped politically by its past role as a British colony. This role has also affected India's current economic status in the world, for better and worse. Finally, Indian culture diffused elements of the British colonial culture, whose footprints are still quite visible. The India of today would be very different without the Britain of its past.

Change over Time Essay Discussion

The Change over Time (COT) essay is scored on a 9-point scale along the following guidelines:

1. Provides an acceptable thesis—1 point
2. Addresses all parts of the question—2 points
3. Supports the thesis with evidence—2 point
4. Uses historical context to show the changes over time—1 point

To earn the remaining three points, the essay must expand beyond these "basic" points, including addressing all parts of the question equally, bringing in outside information, and showing especially insightful analysis. The sample essay provided is an example of a high-scoring essay that accomplishes many of these things. Let's look at it in depth.

The first point of every AP World History scoring rubric comes from the thesis. Likewise, it should be the first goal of every student to draft an introductory paragraph with a comprehensive (and analytical) thesis. Let's look at the thesis paragraph from the sample essay:

Thesis Paragraph:
The impact of colonialism on India has been a dramatic one. Modern India has been shaped politically by its past role as a British colony. This role has also affected India's current economic status in the world, for better and worse. Finally, Indian culture diffused elements of the British colonial culture, whose footprints are still quite visible. In short, <u>colonialism changed India tremendously between 1750 and today in political, economic, and cultural ways.</u>

The thesis statement has been underlined. This introductory paragraph tells the reader what the argument is ("colonialism changed India") and gives a glimpse of the direction the rest of the essay will go. Each of the three key points (politics, economics, and culture) will become the topic of one of the body paragraphs.

The second point of the rubric comes from addressing all parts of the question, though they do not need to be addressed equally. In this case, Indian history must be examined at the beginning of the period (1750), at one or more intermediate stops (e.g., 1857) and at the end (the present). In a paragraph about the Indian economy, each of these periods should be discussed in order. It is vital that students NOT simply give a "snap-shot" of 1750 and of the present and leave it up to the reader to conclude what caused those changes. This is where the fourth point of the rubric comes in.

Demonstrating "historical context" to show change or a lack of change means explaining how and why the historical river flowed over this particular topic. For example:

Historical Context Paragraph:

In 1750, India was one of the world's leading manufacturing centers. Indian textiles, especially cotton, were prized from Beijing to Jenne. With the increasing control of the British East India Company and the British government, however, the Indian economy began to de-industrialize. By the time of the Sepoy Revolt in 1857, India's economy had become largely dedicated to producing raw cotton, which was exported to mills in Manchester and Leeds. The relationship grew even closer once the American Civil War (1860–1865) took the American cotton supply out of British hands. India has not yet regained its status as a manufacturing power, but since its independence in 1948 it has grown as a force in the global economy.

Each segment of change or continuity must involve an explanation by the student of what forces led to these developments. In particular, students should try to make connections between global and regional developments.

The third point of the rubric is often the most difficult for students. It's one thing to say things changed or stayed the same, but it's quite another to offer proof (i.e., historical substantiation). Read the following statements and determine which you think would be most effective in this essay.

- India's economy today is very different than it used to be.
- India's economy has changed in many ways, including its export activity.
- India's economy has changed in many ways, including its export activity. Today, one of its key exports is computer software, thanks in part to the millions of Indians who speak English.

Obviously, the third statement is the best of the bunch. The key is not its length, but the specific evidence it cites. It backs up the idea (the Indian economy has changed) with an example (export activity) and specific information (India's output of computer software.) How many examples, and how much specific information, can you muster for each idea you put forth? The first statement above is woefully inadequate, and the second is not much better. The third is headed in the right direction, but could be even better. Consider the following:

Historical Substantiation Paragraph:

In 1750, India was one of the world's leading manufacturing centers, along with China. Indian textiles, especially cotton, were prized from Beijing to Jenne. With the increasing control of the British East India Company and the British government, however, the Indian economy began to de-industrialize. By the time of the Sepoy Revolt in 1857, India's economy had become largely dedicated to producing raw cotton, which would be exported to mills in Manchester and Leeds. The relationship with England grew even closer once the American Civil War (1860–1865) took the American cotton supply out of British hands. Indian has not yet regained its status as a manufacturing power, but since its independence in 1948 it has grown as a force in the global economy. Today, one of India's main exports is computer software. India can produce this cutting-edge technology because it has many educated citizens, most of whom speak English. In fact, many American companies like General Electric now have customer service call centers in India. These changes are the result of both regional and global factors. Since independence, Indians have reasserted their economic might along with their political freedom. When Indians have controlled their own destiny, they have been quite successful.

This time, there is much more historical substantiation to back up the argument.

Finally, a word about the conclusion paragraph: a good writer not only signals where he or she is going with an introductory paragraph and thesis but also restates the thesis and main points at the end of the essay. This will remind the reader of what you were saying in case you (or they) "wandered off" during the writing/reading. Begin by restating the thesis, as it's your central argument. Then restate your key points. Do not include any new information in this paragraph. If there was information that could have supported your ideas, it should be up in the body of your essay. Also, if you are running short of time you might consider simply restating your thesis as your conclusion paragraph. It will be less effective, but may save you precious time. In a worst-case scenario, you can skip the conclusion completely, as it won't normally be gaining you any points anyway. However, this is only a strategy that is acceptable in a timed essay, such as the one on the AP World History exam. Also, some students find (especially if they didn't pre-write well) that they don't "find" their thesis until they've put all their ideas on the paper, to see where they lead. This is another advantage of having a conclusion paragraph, as the rubric doesn't state that your thesis has to be at the beginning of the paper. It is far better, however, to spend a few minutes pre-writing, and planning your essay and your thesis, than waiting for the end. There's always the possibility that you'll get to the end and find that you still don't have a proper thesis.

Question 3: Comparison

Sample Essay Response

While Constantinople and Timbuktu were two important centers of trade in the period 600 C.E. to 1450, their similarities end there. Constantinople was central to the Eurasian trade routes of the era, whereas Timbuktu was on the fringe of the world trading system. As a result, there were many peoples and cultures represented in Constantinople, whereas Timbuktu had fewer influences. The products for trade in these cities were as different as their geographies would suggest. In other words, the differences between Constantinople and Timbuktu outweighed their similarities, especially with regard to their roles in world trade, their diversity, and their goods.

Constantinople was originally a Greek fishing village called Byzantium. In 324, the Roman Emperor Constantine chose it as the Eastern capital of the Roman Empire and named the city after himself. Timbuktu, on the other hand, began as an oasis for nomadic peoples near the Niger River and was not truly founded until c. 1000 C.E. It grew quickly, however, until it became one of the most important cities in the empires of Ghana (c. 700–100 C.E.) and later Mali (c. 1000–1400). During this era, Constantinople was at the heart of the world trade system. It was close enough to the old Silk Roads to be involved in that trade. Yet it also saw peoples from Russia and Scandinavia trade down the Russian rivers to the Black Sea. Being on a peninsula and the Straits of Bosporus, the city was ideally situated to take in land trade between Europe and Asia and water trade between the Black, Aegean, and Mediterranean seas. For centuries, the Byzantine coin, the Bezant, was an accepted currency across Eurasia. Timbuktu, in contrast, was only peripheral to world trade. Merchants had to cross the Sahara to get there, a trip which could take over two months. The use of camels, brought from the Middle East, greatly expanded the ability of merchants to make the crossing, but it was still a far-flung outpost compared to Baghdad or Constantinople

As a result of their respective geographies, the two cities were quite different in their levels of diversity. Constantinople was mostly a Greek city, but as a former capital of the Roman Empire it had many Latin influences. It was also close enough to the Middle East to have a distinctive Persian element to its culture, such as the custom of separating men and women in church. Hellenized peoples from Egypt and Syria, along with Europeans, Russians, and Muslims (such as Ibn Battuta) could all be found in the city's streets. As all of these people came to trade, they could all be found in the varying "quarters" of the city. Timbuktu, however, was much harder to get to. Its population was mostly African, i.e., peoples of the empire of Ghana and later Mali and some surrounding areas. Muslims came in greater numbers from North Africa and the Middle East, especially after Mansa Musa's hajj to Mecca in 1324–1325. Yet despite its ever-growing influence as an economic, cultural, and even religious center (it had several universities and many mosques by 1450) its level of cultural diversity was much less than that of Constantinople. There were, however, some similarities between the two cities. Obviously, both relied heavily on the Islamic world for trade goods during most of this period. Both were capitals of their respective empires, economically and culturally, as well as politically. Finally, Islamic forces captured both cities: Constantinople in 1453 (by the Ottoman Turks) and Timbuktu in 1590 (by Muslims from Morocco).

The third key difference between the two cities was in the goods in which each city traded. Constantinople's wealth was based on silk, Persian rugs, Indian gems, Russian honey and timber, as well as furs and spices from Eastern Asia. Goods of this sort also arrived from the north and occasionally Europe as well. Timbuktu, on the other hand, dealt largely in gold. The Niger River was a great source of gold for West Africa, so much so that the people there were willing to trade it for salt. Salt was necessary for human survival, and was hard to come by in the area, but it was readily available from the Mediterranean coast. Slaves and ivory were also exchanged for textiles and other manufactured goods from the Middle East and beyond. These exchanges clearly show how both cities were involved in the nearly global trade of the time period. Like all great trading cities, both were also centers for cultural exchange and were much more cosmopolitan than the surrounding countryside. In an era that saw the end of the Roman trade with the East, the rise of Islam, and the Pax Mongolica, these two cities thrived off their commercial successes.

In conclusion, the differences between Constantinople and Timbuktu outweighed their similarities, especially with regard to their roles in world trade, their diversity, and their goods. Constantinople was central to the Eurasian trade routes of the era, whereas Timbuktu was on the fringe of the world trading system. As a result, although there were many peoples and cultures represented in Constantinople, Timbuktu had fewer influences. Finally, the products for trade in these cities were as different as their geographies would suggest. Both cities, however, were important centers of trade in the period 600 C.E. to 1450.

Comparison Essay Discussion

The Comparison Essay is scored on a 9-point scale along the following guidelines:

1. Provides an acceptable thesis—1 point
2. Addresses all parts of the question—2 points
3. Supports the thesis with evidence—2 point
4. Makes one or two direct comparisons—1 point

To earn the remaining three points, the essay must expand beyond these "basic" points, including addressing all parts of the question equally, relating comparisons to a larger global context, bringing in outside information, and showing especially insightful analysis. The sample essay provided is an example of a high-scoring essay that accomplishes many of these things. Let's look at it in depth.

The Thesis Paragraph: The first point of every AP World History rubric comes from the thesis. Thus, it should be the first goal of every student to draft an introductory paragraph with an adequate thesis.

Let's look at the thesis paragraph from the sample essay:

> **Thesis Paragraph:**
> *While Constantinople and Timbuktu were two important centers of trade in the period 600 C.E. to 1450, their similarities end there. Constantinople was central to the Eurasian trade routes of the era, whereas Timbuktu was on the fringe of the world trading system. As a result, there were many peoples and cultures represented in Constantinople, whereas Timbuktu had fewer influences. The products for trade in these cities were as different as their geographies would suggest. <u>The differences between Constantinople and Timbuktu outweighed their similarities, especially with regard to their roles in world trade, their diversity, and their goods.</u>*

The thesis statement has been underlined. This introductory paragraph tells the reader what the argument is ("Constantinople and Timbuktu were more different than similar") and gives a glimpse of the direction the rest of the essay will go. Each of the three key points (centrality to world trade, diversity, and goods) will become the topic of one of the body paragraphs.

Comparison Paragraphs: The second point of the rubric comes from addressing all parts of the question. In this case, a comparison of two cities must be made, involving similarities and differences. The comparison needs to focus on the time period specified (600 C.E.–1450) and discuss economic and non-economic factors. In a paragraph about the centrality of Constantinople and Timbuktu to the world trading system, for example, both cities must be discussed (see the paragraphs cited below). It is vital that students NOT simply discuss one of the two cities, or that they only be discussed briefly. This is where the fourth point of the rubric comes in.

Demonstrating "relevant, direct comparisons" to show similarity and/or difference means being specific and discussing both items. Some students tend to say, "apples are different from oranges because apples have thin peels and are 'meaty.'" This provides insight into the apple, but doesn't say anything about the orange. In the case of this essay question, consider this example:

> **Comparison Paragraph:**
> *A key difference between the two cities was in the goods in which each dealt. Constantinople's wealth was based on goods that arrived mostly from Asia, or from the North and occasionally Europe, as well. Timbuktu, on the other hand, dealt largely with the North African coast. Other goods from the Middle East and beyond were also available.*

The "relevant, direct comparison" has been underlined. Each example of a comparison should take up a paragraph. Smaller examples can be grouped together. In particular, students should try to make connections between global and regional developments. It is also advisable to argue in favor of either similarity or difference, but to spend at least some time acknowledging the option not chosen. No two things are completely alike, or completely different. While each student must choose whether to compare similarities or differences, there is a point available in the "Expanded" section for showing the ability to recognize the "opposite" of the thesis. As a general rule, this section should be brief, so as not to detract from the overall thesis.

Historical Substantiation: Finally, the third point of the rubric is often the most difficult for students. It's one thing to say things were similar or different, it's quite another to offer proof—i.e., historical substantiation. Read the following statements and determine which you think would be most effective in this essay.

- Constantinople was a very diverse city.
- Constantinople was a very diverse city because it had Greek as well as Roman and Persian influence.
- Constantinople was mostly a Greek city, but as a former capital of the Roman Empire it had many Latin influences. It was also close enough to the Middle East to have a distinctive Persian element to its culture, such as the custom of separating men and women in church.

Obviously, the third statement is the best of the bunch. The key is not its length but the specific evidence it cites. It backs up the idea (Constantinople was diverse) with an example (Greek, Roman, and Persian influence) and specific information (women were separated from men during prayer). This, of course, presents the student with his or her greatest challenge. How many examples, and how much specific information, can you muster for each idea you put forth? The first statement above is woefully inadequate, and the second is not much better. The third is headed in the right direction, but it could be even better. Consider the following:

Historical Substantiation Paragraph:

As a result of their respective geographies, the two cities were quite different in their levels of diversity. Constantinople was mostly a Greek city, but as a former capital of the Roman Empire, it had many Latin influences. It was also close enough to the Middle East to have a distinctive Persian element to its culture, such as the custom of separating men and women in church. Hellenized peoples from Egypt and Syria, along with Europeans, Russians, and Muslims (such as Ibn Batuta) could all be found in the city's streets. As all of these people came to trade, they could all be found in the varying "quarters" of the city. Timbuktu, however was much harder to get to. Its population was mostly African—i.e., peoples of the empire of Ghana, and later Mali and some surrounding areas. Muslims came in greater numbers from North Africa and the Middle East, especially after Mansa Musa's hajj to Mecca, in 1324–1325. Yet despite its ever-growing influence as an economic, cultural, and even religious center (it had several universities and many mosques by 1450) its level of cultural diversity was much less than that of Constantinople. There were, however some similarities between the two cities. Obviously, both relied heavily on the Islamic world for trade goods during most of this period. Both were capitals of their respective empires, economically and culturally, as well as politically. Finally, Islamic forces captured both cities: Constantinople in 1453 (by the Ottoman Turks) and Timbuktu in 1590 (by Muslims from Morocco).

This time, there is much more historical substantiation to back up the argument.

Finally, a word about the conclusion paragraph: a good writer not only signals where he or she is going with an introductory paragraph and thesis, but restates the thesis and main points at the end of the essay. This will remind the reader of what you were saying in case you (or they) "wandered off" during the writing/reading. Begin by restating the thesis, as it's your central argument. Then restate your key points. Do not include any new information in this paragraph. If there was information that could have supported your ideas, it should be up in the body of your essay. Also, if you are running short of time, you might consider simply restating your thesis as your conclusion paragraph. It will be less effective, but it may save you precious time. In a worst-case scenario, you can skip the conclusion completely, as it won't normally be gaining you any points anyway. However, this is only a strategy that is acceptable in a timed essay, such as the one on the AP World History Exam.

PRACTICE EXAM 2

AP WORLD HISTORY PRACTICE EXAM 2 ANSWER SHEET

1. Ⓐ Ⓑ Ⓒ Ⓓ Ⓔ	19. Ⓐ Ⓑ Ⓒ Ⓓ Ⓔ	37. Ⓐ Ⓑ Ⓒ Ⓓ Ⓔ	55. Ⓐ Ⓑ Ⓒ Ⓓ Ⓔ
2. Ⓐ Ⓑ Ⓒ Ⓓ Ⓔ	20. Ⓐ Ⓑ Ⓒ Ⓓ Ⓔ	38. Ⓐ Ⓑ Ⓒ Ⓓ Ⓔ	56. Ⓐ Ⓑ Ⓒ Ⓓ Ⓔ
3. Ⓐ Ⓑ Ⓒ Ⓓ Ⓔ	21. Ⓐ Ⓑ Ⓒ Ⓓ Ⓔ	39. Ⓐ Ⓑ Ⓒ Ⓓ Ⓔ	57. Ⓐ Ⓑ Ⓒ Ⓓ Ⓔ
4. Ⓐ Ⓑ Ⓒ Ⓓ Ⓔ	22. Ⓐ Ⓑ Ⓒ Ⓓ Ⓔ	40. Ⓐ Ⓑ Ⓒ Ⓓ Ⓔ	58. Ⓐ Ⓑ Ⓒ Ⓓ Ⓔ
5. Ⓐ Ⓑ Ⓒ Ⓓ Ⓔ	23. Ⓐ Ⓑ Ⓒ Ⓓ Ⓔ	41. Ⓐ Ⓑ Ⓒ Ⓓ Ⓔ	59. Ⓐ Ⓑ Ⓒ Ⓓ Ⓔ
6. Ⓐ Ⓑ Ⓒ Ⓓ Ⓔ	24. Ⓐ Ⓑ Ⓒ Ⓓ Ⓔ	42. Ⓐ Ⓑ Ⓒ Ⓓ Ⓔ	60. Ⓐ Ⓑ Ⓒ Ⓓ Ⓔ
7. Ⓐ Ⓑ Ⓒ Ⓓ Ⓔ	25. Ⓐ Ⓑ Ⓒ Ⓓ Ⓔ	43. Ⓐ Ⓑ Ⓒ Ⓓ Ⓔ	61. Ⓐ Ⓑ Ⓒ Ⓓ Ⓔ
8. Ⓐ Ⓑ Ⓒ Ⓓ Ⓔ	26. Ⓐ Ⓑ Ⓒ Ⓓ Ⓔ	44. Ⓐ Ⓑ Ⓒ Ⓓ Ⓔ	62. Ⓐ Ⓑ Ⓒ Ⓓ Ⓔ
9. Ⓐ Ⓑ Ⓒ Ⓓ Ⓔ	27. Ⓐ Ⓑ Ⓒ Ⓓ Ⓔ	45. Ⓐ Ⓑ Ⓒ Ⓓ Ⓔ	63. Ⓐ Ⓑ Ⓒ Ⓓ Ⓔ
10. Ⓐ Ⓑ Ⓒ Ⓓ Ⓔ	28. Ⓐ Ⓑ Ⓒ Ⓓ Ⓔ	46. Ⓐ Ⓑ Ⓒ Ⓓ Ⓔ	64. Ⓐ Ⓑ Ⓒ Ⓓ Ⓔ
11. Ⓐ Ⓑ Ⓒ Ⓓ Ⓔ	29. Ⓐ Ⓑ Ⓒ Ⓓ Ⓔ	47. Ⓐ Ⓑ Ⓒ Ⓓ Ⓔ	65. Ⓐ Ⓑ Ⓒ Ⓓ Ⓔ
12. Ⓐ Ⓑ Ⓒ Ⓓ Ⓔ	30. Ⓐ Ⓑ Ⓒ Ⓓ Ⓔ	48. Ⓐ Ⓑ Ⓒ Ⓓ Ⓔ	66. Ⓐ Ⓑ Ⓒ Ⓓ Ⓔ
13. Ⓐ Ⓑ Ⓒ Ⓓ Ⓔ	31. Ⓐ Ⓑ Ⓒ Ⓓ Ⓔ	49. Ⓐ Ⓑ Ⓒ Ⓓ Ⓔ	67. Ⓐ Ⓑ Ⓒ Ⓓ Ⓔ
14. Ⓐ Ⓑ Ⓒ Ⓓ Ⓔ	32. Ⓐ Ⓑ Ⓒ Ⓓ Ⓔ	50. Ⓐ Ⓑ Ⓒ Ⓓ Ⓔ	68. Ⓐ Ⓑ Ⓒ Ⓓ Ⓔ
15. Ⓐ Ⓑ Ⓒ Ⓓ Ⓔ	33. Ⓐ Ⓑ Ⓒ Ⓓ Ⓔ	51. Ⓐ Ⓑ Ⓒ Ⓓ Ⓔ	69. Ⓐ Ⓑ Ⓒ Ⓓ Ⓔ
16. Ⓐ Ⓑ Ⓒ Ⓓ Ⓔ	34. Ⓐ Ⓑ Ⓒ Ⓓ Ⓔ	52. Ⓐ Ⓑ Ⓒ Ⓓ Ⓔ	70. Ⓐ Ⓑ Ⓒ Ⓓ Ⓔ
17. Ⓐ Ⓑ Ⓒ Ⓓ Ⓔ	35. Ⓐ Ⓑ Ⓒ Ⓓ Ⓔ	53. Ⓐ Ⓑ Ⓒ Ⓓ Ⓔ	
18. Ⓐ Ⓑ Ⓒ Ⓓ Ⓔ	36. Ⓐ Ⓑ Ⓒ Ⓓ Ⓔ	54. Ⓐ Ⓑ Ⓒ Ⓓ Ⓔ	

AP WORLD HISTORY

Three hours and 5 minutes are allotted for this examination: 55 minutes for Section I, which consists of multiple-choice questions, and 2 hours and 10 minutes for Section II, which consists of essay questions. 10 minutes of Section II are devoted to a mandatory reading period, primarily for the document-based essay question in Part A. Section I is printed in this examination booklet. Section II is printed in a separate booklet. In determining your grade, the two sections are given equal weight.

SECTION I

Time—55 minutes
Number of questions—70
Percent of total grade—50

Section I of this examination contains 70 multiple-choice questions. Therefore, please be careful to fill in only the ovals that are preceded by numbers 1 through 70 on your answer sheet.

General Instructions

INDICATE ALL YOUR ANSWERS TO QUESTIONS IN SECTION I ON THE SEPARATE ANSWER SHEET. No credit will be given for anything written in this examination booklet, but you may use the booklet for notes or scratchwork. After you have decided which of the suggested answers is best, COMPLETELY fill in the corresponding oval on the answer sheet. Give only one answer to each question. If you change an answer, be sure that the previous mark is erased completely.

Example   Sample Answer

Chicago is a   Ⓐ Ⓑ Ⓒ ⬤ Ⓔ

    (A)   state
    (B)   continent
    (C)   country
    (D)   city
    (E)   village

Many candidates wonder whether or not to guess the answers to questions about which they are not certain. In this section of the examination, as a correction for haphazard guessing, one-fourth of the number of questions you answer incorrectly will be subtracted from the number of questions you answer correctly. It is improbable, therefore, that mere guessing will improve your score significantly; it may even lower your score, and it does take time. If, however, you are not sure of the best answer but have some knowledge of the question and are able to eliminate one or more of the answer choices as wrong, your chance of getting the right answer is improved, and it may be to your advantage to answer such a question.

Use your time effectively, working as rapidly as you can without losing accuracy. Do not spend too much time on questions that are too difficult. Go on to other questions and come back to the difficult ones later if you have time. It is not expected that everyone will be able to answer all the multiple-choice questions.

SECTION I: MULTIPLE-CHOICE QUESTIONS

Time—55 minutes

70 Questions

Directions: Each of the questions or incomplete statements below is followed by five suggested answers or completions. Select the one that is best in each case and then fill in the corresponding oval on the answer sheet.

Note: This examination uses the chronological designations B.C.E. (before the Common Era) and C.E. (Common Era). These labels correspond to B.C. (before Christ) and A.D. (anno Domini), which are used in some world history textbooks.

1. [A father said,] "Bring me a fruit from this banyan tree."

    "Here it is, father."

    "Break it."

    "It is broken, Sir."

    "What do you see in it?"

    "Very small seeds, Sir."

    "Break one of them, my son."

    "It is broken, Sir."

    "What do you see in it?"

    "Nothing at all, Sir."

    Then his father spoke to him: "My son, from the very essence in the seed which you cannot see comes in truth this vast banyan tree.

    "Believe me, my son, an invisible and subtle essence is the Spirit of the whole universe. That is reality. That is Atman. THOU ART THAT."

    From the Chandogya Upanishad.

    The quote above refers to which of the following?

    (A) The Confucian belief in the Five Relationships
    (B) The Hindu belief in Brahman, or the universal spirit
    (C) The Hindu belief in reincarnation
    (D) The Taoist teaching on balance in nature
    (E) The Jewish teaching regarding covenants between humans and God

2. According to Jewish tradition, all of the following pairs enacted covenants EXCEPT

    (A) Adam and God
    (B) David and God
    (C) Noah and God
    (D) Abraham and God
    (E) Moses and God

3. What do the Nile, Tigris, Euphrates, Indus, and Yellow rivers have in common? All

    (A) are located in the Fertile Crescent
    (B) were located within the earliest Chinese empires
    (C) overflow their banks with predictable regularity
    (D) gave rise to religions that stressed reincarnation
    (E) were sites of Neolithic, sedentary settlements

4. Which of the following areas was NOT conquered by Alexander the Great?

    (A) Arabia
    (B) Persia
    (C) Greece
    (D) Egypt
    (E) Bactria

GO ON TO THE NEXT PAGE

AP WORLD HISTORY MULTIPLE-CHOICE QUESTIONS

5. From which geographical direction did Buddhism arrived in Southeast Asia? From the

    (A) west and north
    (B) west and south
    (C) east and north
    (D) east and south
    (E) north and south

6. Which of the following describes a characteristic of both Mayan and Egyptian civilizations?

    (A) The belief that the ruler was a god
    (B) The building of pyramids
    (C) Each founded roughly third century B.C.E.
    (D) The belief in monotheism
    (E) The development of the wheel

7.   Silk   Spices   Pearls

    Which of the following best describes these goods in the early part of the 600 C.E. to 1450 era? All were

    (A) exported goods made in China
    (B) luxury items traded over vast distances
    (C) goods traded across the Silk Road, from west to east
    (D) African contributions to the Indian Ocean trade
    (E) the most heavily taxed items by the Chinese Han dynasty

GO ON TO THE NEXT PAGE

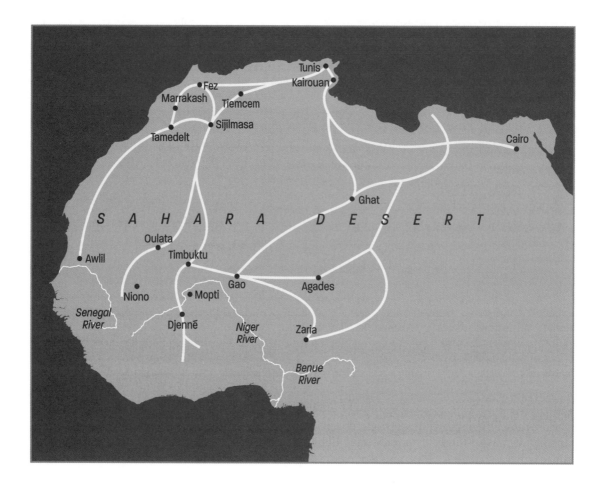

8. Which of the following is most clearly shown by the map above?

    (A) Most trans-Saharan trade was conducted by Muslims.
    (B) The Islamic religion reached Southern Africa over these trade routes.
    (C) Porcelain and silk were prized commodities over these trade routes.
    (D) Timbuktu was the most popular destination of trans-Saharan merchants.
    (E) Camels were a major benefit to merchants on these trade routes.

GO ON TO THE NEXT PAGE

AP WORLD HISTORY MULTIPLE-CHOICE QUESTIONS

9. Which of the following empires had to deal with a controversy surrounding religious icons?

   (A) The empire of Alexander the Great
   (B) The Byzantine Empire
   (C) The Mongol Empire
   (D) The Egyptian Empire
   (E) The Gupta Empire

10. Which of the following describes both the Mongols and the Turks? Both

   (A) converted almost exclusively to Islam
   (B) were heavily recruited into the service of the Abbasid Caliphate
   (C) borrowed siege technology from the Chinese
   (D) conquered the Russian cities of Moscow, Kiev, and Novgorod
   (E) were pastoralists who conquered sedentary civilizations that bordered their lands

11. "Pax Mongolica" can best be described as which of the following?

   (A) The method of terror employed by the Mongols to encourage enemies to surrender
   (B) The diseases, including the Bubonic plague, unknowingly carried by the Mongol invaders
   (C) The peaceful coexistence of various religions within the Mongol empire
   (D) The trade routes that ran through the Mongol empire at its height
   (E) A period of peace established by the Mongols, during which all forms of trade flourished

12. Which of the following describes a way in which European serfs and slaves were different?

   (A) Only Christians could be serfs, whereas only non-Christians could be slaves.
   (B) Serfs were generally unskilled tenant farmers, whereas slaves were usually highly skilled.
   (C) Serfs were exclusively farmers, whereas slaves did exclusively non-agricultural work.
   (D) Only the lands of the Franks had serfs; slaves were used everywhere else in Europe.
   (E) Serfs could not be sold or purchased individually, unlike slaves.

13. Which of the following was acquired by Muslims from the Chinese at the Battle of Talas River in 751 C.E.?

   (A) Gunpowder technology
   (B) The magnetic compass
   (C) Paper-making technology
   (D) Tea-brewing techniques
   (E) Silk-weaving techniques

14. Which of the following explains why the Church rejected the theory of a solar-centered universe as suggested by Nicholas Copernicus?

   (A) Copernicus was a Jew and therefore could not be trusted to report findings accurately.
   (B) The theory contradicted Church teachings regarding an Earth-centered universe.
   (C) A calendar based on the sun was too much like the pagan calendars of the Romans.
   (D) Copernicus was a supporter of Martin Luther and therefore disgraced in the eyes of the Church.
   (E) The theory conflicted with that of the pope, who was also an astronomer.

15. In which of the following ways were slavery in the Islamic Middle East and slavery in the colonies of the New World similar?

   (A) The children of slaves were not slaves themselves.
   (B) Slaves were traded by other Africans for manufactured goods.
   (C) Most slaves did domestic work or were concubines.
   (D) Upon purchase, slaves were forcibly converted to the master's religion.
   (E) The demand for slaves had a devastating impact on Africa's east and west coast populations.

GO ON TO THE NEXT PAGE →

AP WORLD HISTORY MULTIPLE-CHOICE QUESTIONS

16. "Akbar viewed tolerance as merely the first stage in a longer strategy to put an end to sectarian divisions in the subcontinent. Blending elements of the many religions with which he was familiar, he invented a new faith, the Din-i-Ilahi, that he believed could be used to unite his Hindu and Muslim subjects. If the adherents of India's diverse religions could be convinced to embrace this common creed, Akbar reasoned, sectarian quarrels and even violent conflict could be brought to an end."

    Peter N. Stearns et.al. *World Civilizations: The Global Experience*
    In which of the following regions did Akbar rule?

    (A) Southeast Asia
    (B) Persia
    (C) Russia
    (D) India
    (E) East Africa

17. Which of the following nations began its voyages of exploration as a result of the efforts of Prince Henry the Navigator?

    (A) Spain
    (B) England
    (C) Portugal
    (D) The Netherlands
    (E) Venice

18. In which of the following ways were the colonies of the Pilgrims at Plymouth and the various conquistador settlements different?

    (A) The Plymouth colony was established to look for spices, whereas the Spanish wanted gold.
    (B) The conquistadors were mostly single men looking to get rich quick, whereas the colonists of Plymouth were mostly families looking to start a new life.
    (C) The conquistadors were far less interested in converting the natives than were the English.
    (D) Spanish colonies were controlled directly by the crown, whereas English colonies were private.
    (E) The societies the conquistadors established were more egalitarian than the societies the Pilgrims established.

© Getty Images

19. Which of the following explains why this style of dress from Japan ceased to be used?

    (A) Climate change made the heavy armor unpractical.
    (B) Industrial production ended the era of handmade armor.
    (C) Guns and commoners as soldiers replaced the skilled warrior.
    (D) The Tokugawa shoguns forbid armor in order to keep the samurai humble.
    (E) Western style pants and coats became the fashion instead of armor.

20. The Ottoman Empire and the Spanish Empire of the period 1450 to 1750 were different in which of the following ways?

    (A) Ottoman trade grew steadily through this period, but Spanish economic power declined.
    (B) Ottoman government was controlled by a council of clerics, but a monarch ruled Spain.
    (C) Ottoman society extended far greater status to women than the Spanish did.
    (D) The Ottomans let Christians and Jews practice their faiths, whereas the Spanish exiled Jews and Muslims.
    (E) Ottoman lands grew through political marriage, whereas Spain chose not to follow this path.

GO ON TO THE NEXT PAGE

AP WORLD HISTORY MULTIPLE-CHOICE QUESTIONS

21. All of the following are reasons why the years around 1450 were a pivotal period EXCEPT

    (A) Europeans began to trade for slaves in Africa
    (B) the Yuan dynasty in China collapsed
    (C) Constantinople fell to the Turks
    (D) the Renaissance in Europe reached its midpoint
    (E) the decline of Kilwa and Great Zimbabwe began

22. In which of the following ways were the goals of Zheng He and European explorers similar?

    (A) Both wanted to discover previously uncharted lands.
    (B) Each was in search of new lands to colonize.
    (C) Both sought precious metals to increase their nations' wealth.
    (D) Each was in search of nonbelievers to convert to their respective religions.
    (E) Both were looking for trade goods not available in their home countries.

23. In which of the following ways were the revolutions in France and Haiti similar?

    (A) In both nations, slavery was a key point of protest.
    (B) Both Haitians and the French citizenry had grown tired of Louis XVI's fiscal mismanagement.
    (C) In both revolutions, a lower class was greatly responsible for the overthrow of the government.
    (D) Both nations' economies had been damaged by an over-reliance on sugar exports.
    (E) Both nations received aid from the newly independent Americans.

24. In which of the following ways did the French Revolution influence the Haitian Revolution?

    (A) The sale of Louisiana by Napoleon spurred the Haitians out of fear they might be sold too.
    (B) The arrival of Napoleon's troops incited the previously loyal Haitians to rebel.
    (C) Most Haitians were loyal to Louis XVI and preferred not to be part of the French Republic.
    (D) French Revolutionary rhetoric spread to the slaves of Haiti.
    (E) French Revolutionary attitudes toward the Church offended the devoutly Catholic Haitians.

25. Which of the following describes a way in which the treatment of Native Americans and native South Africans was similar?

    (A) Both were forcibly converted to Christianity by zealous Europeans.
    (B) Each was forced into mine or plantation labor gangs to serve European companies.
    (C) Both were forcibly moved to areas reserved for them while their former land was confiscated.
    (D) Both were given only token representation in local or provincial governments.
    (E) Both were exiled by Europeans from their native countries to surrounding nations.

26. All of the following are reasons why the Industrial Revolution began in Britain EXCEPT

    (A) Britain had the oldest and most renowned universities and research centers in Europe
    (B) the Anglican Church had not stood in the way of science or technological development
    (C) the British government gave citizens more political and economic rights and flexibility
    (D) a boom in agricultural advances boosted both food production and population needed for a large labor force
    (E) the British government enacted policies that increased the urban labor force for factories

27. Which of the following describes one of the outcomes of the Opium Wars?

    (A) Britain received Hong Kong and surrounding territories as exclusive territory.
    (B) Britain agreed to cease the importation of opium into China.
    (C) British citizens were forcibly expelled from all of China.
    (D) All of China became a protectorate of the British Empire, except Taiwan.
    (E) China agreed to give complete access to all territories to Christian missionaries.

GO ON TO THE NEXT PAGE

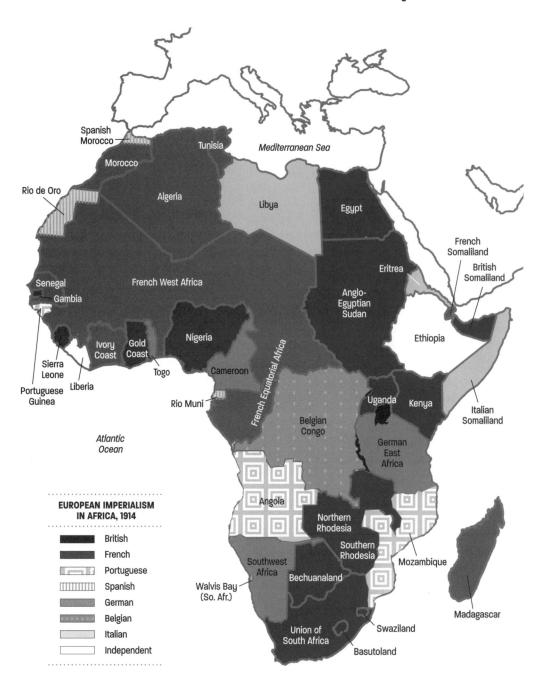

EUROPEAN IMPERIALISM
IN AFRICA, 1914

British
French
Portuguese
Spanish
German
Belgian
Italian
Independent

28. Which of the following explains why there were so relatively few Italian colonies in Africa?

(A) Most of Italy's colonial efforts were focused on Asia and the islands of the Pacific.
(B) Italy did not become a nation until the 1870s, by which time most of Africa had been claimed.
(C) Italy was sufficiently rich in resources, so colonization was not a priority.
(D) The devout Catholicism of Italy's early leaders discouraged the conquest of other peoples.
(E) The Italian military was required to focus on frequent skirmishes with the Ottoman Empire.

GO ON TO THE NEXT PAGE

29. Which of the following accurately describes some of the Allied and Central Powers of World War I?

    (A) Allied—France, Germany, Britain; Central—Austria, Russia, Turkey, Italy
    (B) Allied—Britain, Germany, Russia; Central—France, Austria, Turkey
    (C) Allied—Britain, France, Turkey; Central—Russia, Germany, Austria
    (D) Allied—Germany, Austria, Turkey; Central—France, Britain, Russia
    (E) Allied—Britain, Russia, France; Central—Germany, Austria, Turkey

30. All of the following were key leaders in the cause for women's rights in the United States and Britain EXCEPT:

    (A) Elizabeth Cady Stanton
    (B) Emmeline Pankhurst
    (C) Marie Curie
    (D) Susan B. Anthony
    (E) Lucretia Mott

31. Which of the following women was not the leader of a modern nation in the twentieth century?

    (A) Golda Meir
    (B) Indira Gandhi
    (C) Margaret Thatcher
    (D) Aung San Su Ky
    (E) Benazir Bhutto

32. Which of the following are modern examples of civil unrest in nations whose borders were drawn so as to include varying ethnicities after colonialism?

    (A) Iran and Japan
    (B) Egypt and Mexico
    (C) Russia and India
    (D) Iraq and Rwanda
    (E) Mexico and India

33. Which of the following nations did Algerians have to fight for their independence?

    (A) Britain
    (B) Italy
    (C) France
    (D) Egypt
    (E) Belgium

34. After the Chinese Communist Revolution, where did the Nationalist (Guomindang) Party members flee?

    (A) Japan
    (B) Korea
    (C) Taiwan
    (D) Hawaii
    (E) Vietnam

35. All of the following were programs or slogans created by Mao Zedong after the Communist Revolution EXCEPT

    (A) the Hundred Schools of Thought
    (B) the Cultural Revolution
    (C) the Great Leap Forward
    (D) Let a Hundred Flowers Bloom
    (E) the Four Olds Campaign

GO ON TO THE NEXT PAGE

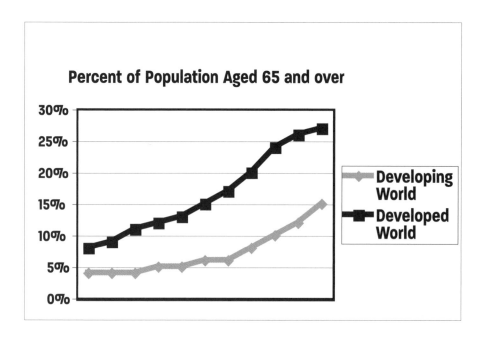

36. Which of the following is a conclusion that can be reached on the basis of the graph above?

(A) People in America are generally younger than those in France.
(B) There are more young people in Cambodia than in Japan.
(C) There are more young people in Britain than in Guatemala.
(D) The populations of industrial nations are generally younger than those in nonindustrial ones.
(E) The populations of developing nations are generally younger than those in developed nations.

GO ON TO THE NEXT PAGE

AP WORLD HISTORY MULTIPLE-CHOICE QUESTIONS

© V. N. O'key

37. Which of the following is depicted in the above photo?

(A) Lions of Emperor Qin
(B) One of the Pillars of Asoka
(C) The Obelisk of Cleopatra
(D) One of the Bronze Tablets of Rome
(E) The capital to a column, containing Hammurabi's Code

38. All of the following occurred during the so-called "Axial Period" EXCEPT

(A) development of Zoroastrianism in Persia
(B) life of the Buddha, in India
(C) life of Confucius, in China
(D) development of Christianity, separate from Judaism
(E) life of Socrates, Plato, and Aristotle, in Greece

39. In which of the following ways were Taoism and Confucianism similar?

(A) Both emphasized the importance of the relationship between ruler and subject.
(B) Each taught that the world was in a balance between diametrically opposing forces.
(C) Both became standard doctrine for rulers in China.
(D) Each was readily exported to Japan through cultural diffusion.
(E) Each sought to bring order to a chaotic society through a unique social order.

40. In which of the following ways were the Huns and Hunas different?

(A) The Huns were mostly farmers, whereas the Hunas were largely pastoralists.
(B) The Huns were constantly hostile to settled peoples, and the Hunas were usually not.
(C) The Huns were polytheistic, whereas the Hunas were early monotheists.
(D) The Huns were from Central Asia, and the Hunas were from Eastern Asia.
(E) The Huns helped destroy the Roman Empire, whereas the Hunas destroyed the Gupta Empire.

41. All of the following were advances made by Islamic science EXCEPT

(A) eye surgery, including removing cataracts
(B) compilation of books detailing medical knowledge
(C) development of lenses, including an early microscope
(D) astronomical advances, including naming many stars
(E) development of algebra and trigonometry

GO ON TO THE NEXT PAGE

42. "Yet their women show no bashfulness before men and do not veil themselves, though they are assiduous in attending the prayers. Any man who wishes to marry one of them may do so, but they do not travel with their husbands, and even if one desired to do so her family would not allow her to go.

    The women there have 'friends' and 'companions' amongst the men outside their own families, and the men in the same way have 'companions' amongst the women of other families. A man may go into his house and find his wife entertaining her 'companion' but he takes no objection to it."

Ibn Battuta. *Travels in Asia and Africa 1325–1354.*

Which of the following is demonstrated by the quote above?

(A) West Africans were not devout Muslims and looked down on by others of their faith.
(B) Islam came to West Africa through trade across the Sahara.
(C) Women of Mali had virtually no personal or political rights.
(D) Religions may change as they are diffused into new regions and cultures.
(E) The introduction of a new religion temporarily destroys a region's social order.

43. Which of the following explains why the Russian word *czar* was derived from the Roman word *Caesar*?

(A) Refugees from Rome settled in the region that became Russia.
(B) Germanic peoples who attacked Rome diffused its culture to Russia.
(C) Roman missionaries on the Silk Road converted the Mongols, who later captured Russia.
(D) Russian wheat merchants dealt extensively with Rome, diffusing cultures and the ruler's title.
(E) Russian culture borrowed from Byzantine culture, including the title for their ruler.

44. Historically, what do Baghdad, Kiev, Samarkand, and Peking all have in common?

(A) All were captured by the Mongols.
(B) All four were on the Silk Road.
(C) Each was an early stronghold of Islam.
(D) Each was depopulated by the bubonic plague.
(E) All four were visited by Marco Polo on his journeys.

45. Which of the following explains why the bubonic plague tended to have a higher mortality rate in cities than in rural areas?

(A) The higher population density of cities made it easier for the plague to affect more people.
(B) City residents tended to live in filthier conditions than the people of the countryside.
(C) Merchants who spread the plague were drawn to cities for trade.
(D) City residents drew from water sources contaminated by the plague.
(E) Missionaries and religious pilgrims spread the plague on their journeys from city to city.

46. Which of the following explains the unique heritage of the Swahili language?

(A) Africans did frequent business with Chinese merchants, creating a hybrid language.
(B) Buddhist merchants from India attempted to convert coastal Africans and created a language.
(C) Arab merchants spread their language and Islam to the coast, creating a new language.
(D) Trade from Central Africa to the coast culturally diffused the two culture groups.
(E) Indonesian sailors brought bananas and their language to the coast of Africa.

GO ON TO THE NEXT PAGE

© Getty Images

47. Which of the following would be an accurate caption for the above picture?

(A) The mosque of Jenne in West Africa symbolizes the spread of Islam across the Sahara.
(B) The mosque of Cairo symbolizes the Mamaluk Empire, which stopped the Mongols.
(C) The mosque of Baghdad was built by the Abbasids to mark their new capital on the trade routes.
(D) The mosque of Mecca houses the Ka'bah, the holiest site in Islam.
(E) The mosque of Delhi was built by the Sultanate of Delhi to inspire Hindu conversions.

GO ON TO THE NEXT PAGE

48.   "Austronesian-speaking peoples possessed a sophisticated maritime technology as well as agricultural expertise, and they established human settlements in the islands of the Pacific Ocean. Their outrigger canoes enabled them to sail safely over long distances of open ocean, and their food crops and domesticated animals enabled them to establish agricultural societies in the islands. Once they had established coastal settlements in New Guinea, Austronesian seafarers sailed easily to the Bismark and Solomon islands, perhaps in the interests of trade. From there they undertook exploratory voyages that led them to previously unpopulated islands."

Jerry H. Bentley and Herbert F. Ziegler. *Traditions and Encounters*.

Which of the following is most clearly demonstrated by the reading above?

(A) Austronesian-speaking peoples created a vast empire through conquest.
(B) Austronesian-speaking peoples created an empire similar to that of the Mongols.
(C) The spread of cultures is most often accomplished through commercial trade.
(D) The migration of peoples has become very difficult since the end of the last Ice Age.
(E) The spread of peoples and cultures includes many components, including behaviors and foods.

49. All of the following went to the Western Hemisphere as a result of the Columbian Exchange EXCEPT

(A) corn (maize)
(B) horses
(C) sheep
(D) wheat
(E) Africans

50. Which of the following best explains why the population of Native Americans dropped rapidly after the arrival of Europeans in the Americas?

(A) Most of them were worked to death in mines and on plantations.
(B) Natives had little resistance to germs that were brought by Europeans.
(C) European military technology was so powerful that it enabled the destruction of whole peoples.
(D) Most natives were taken back to Africa or Europe as slaves.
(E) Rather than fight the Europeans, most natives emigrated to Asia by boat or land bridge.

51.   Silk   Sugar   Spices   Gold   Porcelain

What did all of the products listed above have in common in the era 1450 to 1750?

(A) They were highly sought after by Europeans, who would sail around Africa to get them.
(B) Europeans prized the products so highly that they destroyed the Ottoman Empire to acquire them.
(C) The control of the trade of these items enabled China to dominate Indian Ocean trade.
(D) Before the Europeans arrived, these products were carried exclusively by armed Muslim ships.
(E) All of these products were for sale in abundance in Japan during this era.

52. Most African slaves had been captured by other African tribes or nations as prisoners of war and then sold into the slave trade. Which of the following explains why Africans assisted the Europeans in this trade instead of resisting the enslavement of any and all Africans?

(A) Africans who converted to Christianity felt a greater loyalty to Europeans than to Africa.
(B) Africans had no resources with which to trade and were otherwise very poor.
(C) African leaders saw guns and slavery as a way to rid themselves of local rivals.
(D) Africans were unaware that the captives were to be taken away, never to return.
(E) Africans envisioned a better life in the New World, even as slaves, than they had in Africa.

GO ON TO THE NEXT PAGE

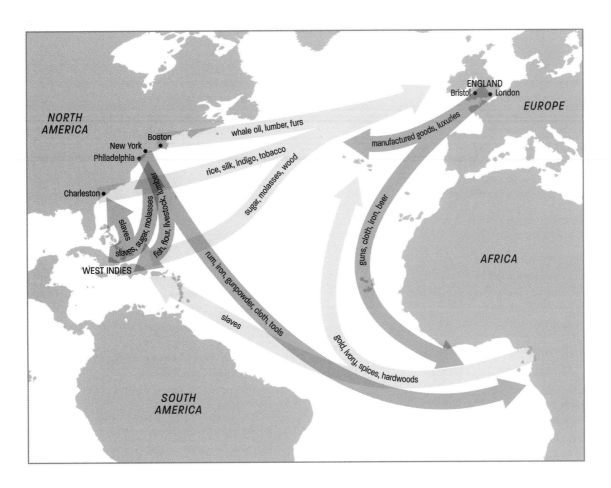

53. The map above demonstrates which of the following about the Atlantic Ocean trade in the period 1450 to 1750?

(A) Europe produced goods not available in the Americas or Africa.

(B) Africa produced mostly manufactured goods, whereas the Americas produced raw materials.

(C) Currents and winds forced most ships to sail north before heading east.

(D) African merchants provided much of the transport necessary for Atlantic trade.

(E) The most important trade item for the West Indies was lumber.

GO ON TO THE NEXT PAGE

54. *Sati* (or *suttee*) can best be described as which of the following?

   (A) An Indian ship, used for trade in coastal waters of the Indian Ocean
   (B) The ritual suicide of some Indian women in their husband's funeral pyres
   (C) A form of currency based on shells, made popular by merchants from Southeast Asia
   (D) A Chinese luxury item, made from sea cucumbers and valued for its medicinal qualities
   (E) A small cannon mounted on the bow of European caravels, which sailed the Indian Ocean

55. Which of the following describes the two key governing instruments of the Ottoman Empire?

   (A) The Shah and the Sultan
   (B) The Sultan and the Caliph
   (C) The Shah and the ulama
   (D) The Sultan and the ulama
   (E) The Sufis and the Shah

56. China and Japan permitted trade with Europeans c. 1760 in which of the following areas?

   (A) Hong Kong and Edo
   (B) Beijing and Tokyo
   (C) Taiwan Island and Deshima Island
   (D) Guangzhou (Canton) and Hiroshima
   (E) Guangzhou (Canton) and Deshima Island

57. Neocolonialism can best be described as which of the following?

   (A) Control of colonies through native rulers who did the bidding of European nations
   (B) Control of areas in the nineteenth century by industrialized nations in search of raw materials
   (C) Conquest of areas in the New World by Europeans, as opposed to colonies in Asia or Africa
   (D) Conquest of developing nations by developed nations with gunpowder technology
   (E) Control of a developing nation through the control of its economy by a developed nation(s)

58. In which of the following ways were the Young Turks and the Meiji Restoration similar?

   (A) Both hoped to give power to an emperor instead of local governors.
   (B) Both sought to modernize their nations to better compete with Europe.
   (C) Both intended to reduce the power of religious officials in government.
   (D) Neither was successful in the long-term achievement of its goals.
   (E) Both were supported by Europeans, so as to weaken the Ottoman government.

59. Which of the following was a result of the Sepoy Revolt in India in 1857?

   (A) Britain gave India its complete independence.
   (B) The French were forced to give up their remaining Indian possessions.
   (C) Cotton was no longer taxed by Indian rajas as it was exported to Britain.
   (D) Hindus came to control the majority of India's provincial governments.
   (E) The control of India by the British East India Company was ended.

60. Which of the following were the French partially responsible for building during the period 1750 to 1914?

   (A) The railways of India and the Eiffel Tower
   (B) The Straits of Malacca and the Golden Gate Bridge
   (C) The Statue of Liberty and the Erie Canal
   (D) The Suez and Panama canals
   (E) The Maginot Line and the Ho Chi Minh Trail

61. All of the following occurred between 1890 and 1930 EXCEPT:

   (A) Japan defeated China in a war, claiming Taiwan.
   (B) Japan defeated Russia in a war, largely through naval power.
   (C) Japan conquered the Philippines.
   (D) Japan conquered Korea and made it a colony.
   (E) Japan signed several naval treaties with the United States and Britain.

GO ON TO THE NEXT PAGE

Immigration to the United States, 1870-1920

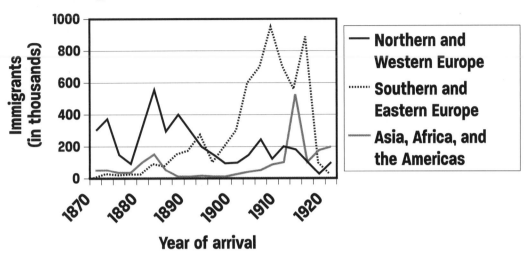

62. Which of the following is an accurate conclusion, based on the graph above?

(A) Most immigrants to America came by way of San Francisco.
(B) More immigrants came to America from France than from Germany.
(C) The majority of immigrants to America came by sailing vessels, not steam ships.
(D) Discrimination prevented most Asian or African immigrants from coming to America.
(E) Immigration to America from southern Europe didn't become extensive until the 1890s.

GO ON TO THE NEXT PAGE

63. Which of the following accurately describes the differences of the colonization of Australia and Singapore? Australia was

   (A) a prison colony, whereas Singapore controlled trade through the Straits of Malacca
   (B) rich with diamonds, whereas Singapore grew wealthy from the rubber trade
   (C) a British colony, whereas Singapore was Japanese
   (D) settled by European Catholics, whereas Protestants settled Singapore
   (E) strategic for trans-Pacific shipping, whereas Singapore was an Indian Ocean port

64. Which of the following explains why the United States was funding military actions in Nicaragua and El Salvador in the 1980s?

   (A) The United States was desperate to secure new reserves of petroleum from Central America.
   (B) The United States revived the Monroe Doctrine, hoping to assert its influence in the hemisphere.
   (C) Dictators in both nations were openly hostile to American foreign policy.
   (D) The United States was attempting to counter communism in those and other nations.
   (E) American fruit companies had been threatened by local militias.

65. Which of the following is an accurate description of women's rights in modern Turkey and Saudi Arabia?

   (A) Turkish women are not allowed to vote, whereas Saudi women have the legal right to do so.
   (B) Turkish women have full political rights and Saudi women do not.
   (C) Both Turkish and Saudi women must wear veils in public and cover their heads.
   (D) Although there are no clothing restrictions, neither Turkish nor Saudi women are allowed to drive.
   (E) Women in both countries must answer to the "religious police" regarding Islamic laws.

66. Which of the following are permanent members of the United Nations' Security Council?

   (A) Britain, the United States, and Germany
   (B) France, China, and Russia
   (C) Japan, Britain, and the United States
   (D) Britain, India, and China
   (E) Russia, Egypt, and Mexico

67. In which of the following ways were the genocides of Stalin and the Khmer Rouge similar? Both were

   (A) intent on creating an agrarian society.
   (B) focused on punishing an ethnic minority.
   (C) the result of religious intolerance.
   (D) the work of Communist regimes.
   (E) done under the direction of the Chinese Communists.

68. Which of the following nations enacted a policy of voluntary sterilization as a means to reduce population growth?

   (A) Egypt
   (B) Mexico
   (C) Indonesia
   (D) India
   (E) Japan

69. Which of the following events caused the United Nations Educational, Scientific and Cultural Organization (UNESCO) to criticize the Taliban regime in Afghanistan?

   (A) Destruction of ancient Buddhist statues
   (B) Prohibitions on free speech over public airwaves
   (C) Destruction of Afghanistan's public and private museums
   (D) Restriction on the rights of women and non-Muslims
   (E) Exportation of opium and other narcotics out of Afghanistan

70. Which of the following best describes the significance of India's "Bollywood" movies?

   (A) India is a contributor to the global culture, similar to but with less impact than the U.S. media.
   (B) Indian nationalists locked in a struggle with Pakistan are motivated by Bollywood films.
   (C) The Indian film industry now accounts for roughly 15 percent of India's Gross Domestic Product.
   (D) The Indian film industry is eliminating languages such as Hindi and Urdu from popular culture.
   (E) Movies depicting Hindu stories have created a resurgence in religion.

END OF SECTION I

AP WORLD HISTORY
SECTION II

You will have 10 minutes to read Section II. You are advised to spend most of the 10 minutes analyzing the documents and planning your answer for the document-based question in Part A. If you have time, you may spend some portion of the time reading the questions in Part B and Part C. At the end of the 10 minutes, you may begin writing your answers. Suggested writing time is 40 minutes for the document-based essay question in Part A. You will have 5 minutes of planning time and 35 minutes of writing time for each essay question in Part B and Part C.

BE SURE TO MANAGE YOUR TIME CAREFULLY

Note: This examination uses the chronological designations B.C.E. (before the common era and C.E. (common era). These labels correspond to B.C. (before Christ) and A.D. (annon Domini), which are used in some world history textbooks.

Part A
(Suggested writing time—40 minutes)
Percent of Section II score—$33\frac{1}{3}$

Directions: The following question is based on the accompanying Documents 1 through 7. (The documents have been edited for the purpose of this excercise.)

This question is designed to test your ability to work with and understand historical documents. Write an essay that:

- has a relevant thesis that is supported by evidence from the documents
- uses all or all but one of the documents
- analyzes the documents by grouping them in as many appropriate ways as possible. **Do not simply summarize the documents individually.**
- takes into account both the sources of the documents and the authors' points of view

You may refer to relevant historical information not mentioned in the documents.

1. Modern Africa is beset by many problems that prevent it from joining the community of prosperous, free nations. Based on the following documents, evaluate the following statement:

   "The problems of modern Africa are largely the result of its history as a possession of Europeans, who have since abandoned it."

   What kinds of additional documents would you need to evaluate this statement?

Document 1

> Source: Excerpt from website of Africa Action, Washington, D.C. 2005.
>
> Africa's debts are owed to the governments of rich countries like the United States and Britain and to international financial institutions like the World Bank and the International Monetary Fund (IMF), which are controlled by these governments. Each year, the poorest countries in Africa are forced to pay more money to these wealthy creditors than they receive in aid or in new loans. This debt gives these foreign creditors great power over Africa's economies and over the continent's future.

GO ON TO THE NEXT PAGE

Document 2

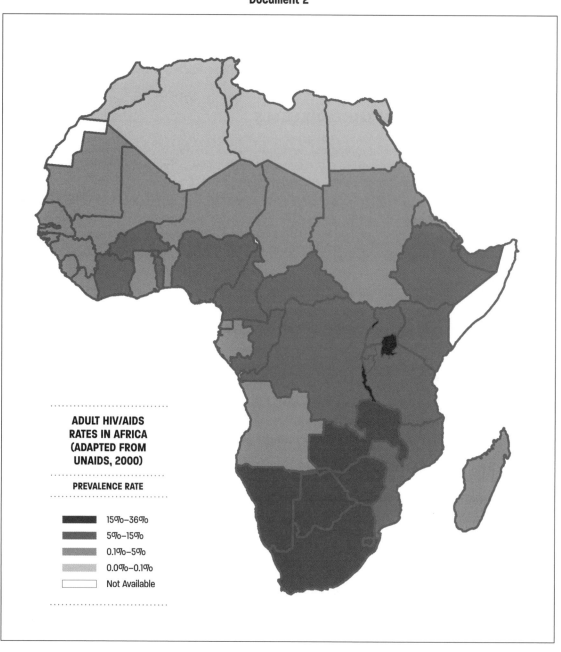

**ADULT HIV/AIDS
RATES IN AFRICA
(ADAPTED FROM
UNAIDS, 2000)**

PREVALENCE RATE

- 15%–36%
- 5%–15%
- 0.1%–5%
- 0.0%–0.1%
- Not Available

GO ON TO THE NEXT PAGE

Document 3

Source: BBC News Report, September 8, 2000.

"You know we can make a real difference and give a fresh start to a billion people who are living on, what is it, less than a dollar a day," [said singer, Bono]

[Bono] told reporters outside: "It's madness that a pop star has to be standing here. Somebody else should be doing this, somebody else more qualified.

"But you know what? They don't have time. They're not bad guys in Washington, they're just busy guys."

The 40-year-old singer is part of the star-studded Jubilee 2000 campaign to bring an end to world debt.

The group is pressing for Western leaders to write off up to and $350 billion in "unpayable" arrears.

After the meeting with [U.N. Secretary General] Kofi Annan, Bono vowed to get debt relief "up the list of priorities."

The world record amount of signatures and thumbprints on the petition were collected from 155 countries and include those of David Bowie, Sir Anthony Hopkins, Muhammad Ali and the Dalai Lama.

Document 4

Source: Amnesty International, 2005.

P.K., now thirteen, was abducted in Liberia in 2002. "Government soldiers came and forced me and my father to join them. My father refused so they cut his throat.

They beat me and tied me and forced me to join the fighters".

Children are recruited because they are perceived as cheap and expendable, easily brutalized into fearless killing and unquestioning obedience. Child soldiers are often chosen for the most dangerous assignments or forced to participate in appalling human rights abuses, sometimes against their own families or communities. Children are also forced to carry ammunition, find and prepare food or perform other noncombat roles.

Document 5

Source: United Nations, 2004.

While the tragedy of the HIV/AIDS epidemic has been drawing increased media attention, one of the most troubling aspects of it has been that the long-term impact on African societies of some 11 million AIDS orphans in sub-Saharan Africa has been featured less often.

There are more than 34 million orphans in the region today and some 11 million of them are orphaned by AIDS. Eight out of every ten children in the world whose parents have died of AIDS live in sub-Saharan Africa. During the last decade, the proportion of children who are orphaned as a result of AIDS rose from 3.5 percent to 32 percent and will continue to increase exponentially as the disease spreads unchecked. As a result, the disease is in effect making orphans of a whole generation of children, jeopardizing their health, their rights, their well-being and sometimes their very survival, not to mention the overall development prospects of their countries.

GO ON TO THE NEXT PAGE

Document 6

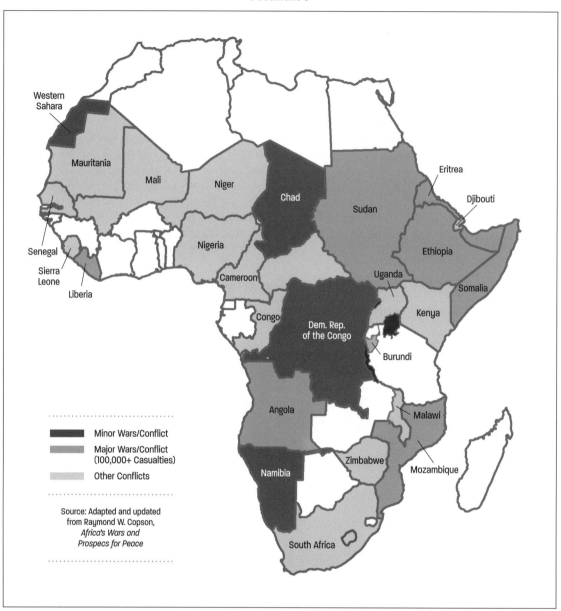

Minor Wars/Conflict

Major Wars/Conflict
(100,000+ Casualties)

Other Conflicts

Source: Adapted and updated
from Raymond W. Copson,
*Africa's Wars and
Prospecs for Peace*

Document 7

Source: U.S. Treasury Secretary Paul O'Neill, May 28, 2002, as reported by BBC News.

"Forty-five percent of the people don't have clean water [and] if you look at the amount of money that's come into Uganda since 1986, I'm continuing to ask the question why clean water was such a low priority that it didn't get funding?"

The amount of money that's required to give everyone here clean water is maybe $25m [million] [but] according to the local people, the World Bank gave them $300m and still getting them clean water was not a high priority."

END OF PART A

GO ON TO THE NEXT PAGE

AP WORLD HISTORY
SECTION II
Part B

(Suggested planning and writing time—40 minutes)
Percent of Section II score—33 $\frac{1}{3}$

Directions: You are to answer the following question. You should spend 5 minutes organizing or outlining your essay. Write an essay that:

- has a relevant thesis and supports that thesis with appropriate historical evidence
- addresses all parts of the question
- uses historical context to show change over time and/or continuities

2. Discuss the change or continuity to the demographics of ONE of the following regions. Focus on the period 1450 to 1914 and include some analysis on the role of disease.

   - Western Europe
   - West Africa
   - Central America
   - The Caribbean

GO ON TO THE NEXT PAGE

AP WORLD HISTORY
SECTION II
Part C

(Suggested planning and writing time—40 minutes)
Percent of Section II score—33 $\frac{1}{3}$

Directions: You are to answer the following question. You should spend 5 minutes organizing or outlining your essay. Write an essay that:

- has a relevant thesis and supports that thesis with appropriate historical evidence
- addresses all parts of the question
- makes direct, relevant comparisons

3. Compare the roles of women in TWO of the following religions. Consider their roles in society as influenced by their faiths, as well as the teaching of each religion.

 - Judaism
 - Buddhism
 - Islam
 - Hinduism

WHEN YOU FINISH WRITING, CHECK YOUR WORK
ON SECTION II IF TIME PERMITS.

END OF EXAMINATION

PRACTICE EXAM 2: ANSWERS & EXPLANATIONS

Answer Key for Practice Exam 2

Number	Answer	Right	Wrong	Number	Answer	Right	Wrong	Number	Answer	Right	Wrong
1	B	___	___	25	C	___	___	49	A	___	___
2	B	___	___	26	A	___	___	50	B	___	___
3	E	___	___	27	A	___	___	51	A	___	___
4	A	___	___	28	B	___	___	52	C	___	___
5	A	___	___	29	E	___	___	53	A	___	___
6	B	___	___	30	C	___	___	54	E	___	___
7	B	___	___	31	D	___	___	55	D	___	___
8	E	___	___	32	D	___	___	56	E	___	___
9	B	___	___	33	C	___	___	57	E	___	___
10	E	___	___	34	C	___	___	58	B	___	___
11	E	___	___	35	A	___	___	59	E	___	___
12	E	___	___	36	E	___	___	60	D	___	___
13	C	___	___	37	B	___	___	61	C	___	___
14	B	___	___	38	D	___	___	62	E	___	___
15	B	___	___	39	E	___	___	63	A	___	___
16	D	___	___	40	E	___	___	64	D	___	___
17	C	___	___	41	C	___	___	65	B	___	___
18	B	___	___	42	D	___	___	66	B	___	___
19	C	___	___	43	E	___	___	67	D	___	___
20	D	___	___	44	A	___	___	68	D	___	___
21	B	___	___	45	A	___	___	69	A	___	___
22	E	___	___	46	C	___	___	70	A	___	___
23	C	___	___	47	A	___	___				
24	D	___	___	48	E	___	___				

HOW TO CALCULATE YOUR SCORE

Section I: Multiple Choice

[_____ − ($\frac{1}{4}$ × _____)] × 0.8571 = _____

Number
Correct
(out of 70)

Number Wrong

Weighted
Section I Score
(Do not round.)

Section II: Free Response

Question 1 _____ × 2.2222 = _____

(out of 9)

Question 2 _____ × 2.2222 = _____

(out of 9)

Question 3 _____ × 2.2222 = _____

(out of 9)

Sum = _____

Weighted
Section II Score
(Do not round.)

Composite Score

_____ + _____ = _____

Weighted Section I
Score

Weighted Section II
Score

Composite Score
(Round to the nearest
whole number.)

Composite Score*	AP Grade	Interpretation
78–120	5	extremely well qualified
62–77	4	well qualified
43–61	3	qualified
27–42	2	possibly qualified
0–26	1	no recommendation

*Each year the Development Committee determines the formulas used to calculate the raw composite scores. The Chief Faculty Consultant determines how the composite scores fit into the 5-point AP scale.

SECTION I: MULTIPLE-CHOICE EXPLANATIONS

1. **B**   Cultural and Intellectual Developments: 8000 B.C.E.–600 C.E.

Hinduism teaches that all things in creation are essentially made of the same "Brahman" or cosmic matter. Reincarnation or creation is simply a refashioning of this material into a new form. Confucianism includes the Father-Son relationship among its Five Relationships, as choice **A** indicates, but that is not what the quote refers to. Likewise, the quote is indirectly addressing an aspect of reincarnation, but not reincarnation directly, as choice **C** states. The balance of Taoism, choice **D**, and the covenants of Judaism, choice **E**, are not addressed at all.

2. **B**   Cultural and Intellectual Developments: 8000 B.C.E.–600 C.E.

A covenant in the Jewish faith is a sacred agreement between humans and God. Adam, choice **A**, agreed not to eat of the tree of knowledge. Noah, choice **C**, agreed to build an ark. Abraham, choice **D**, agreed to worship God in return for the Promised Land and his descendents being named as God's chosen people. Moses, choice **E**, agreed to lead the Israelites out of Egypt. David, while a victor in battle, a composer of Psalms, and a king, did not have an agreement with God, making choice **B** the correct answer.

3. **E**   The Relationship of Change and Continuity: 8000 B.C.E.–600 C.E.

All the earliest sites of Neolithic settlement were on alluvial rivers—rivers that regularly overflowed their banks and naturally irrigated the land, providing for excellent farming, as indicated in choice **E**. Though each of the rivers listed regularly overflowed their banks, only the Nile did so with any predictable consistency. Thus, though a close second, option **C**, is not the BEST answer. Only the Tigris and Euphrates are located in the Fertile Crescent, as choice **A** indicates, and only the Yellow River was located near a Chinese empire, as in choice **B**. All alluvial river civilizations did give rise to religions that believed in an afterlife—with the yearly "rebirth" of the land, it's no wonder. Reincarnation however, as in choice **D**, was a concept unique to India.

4. **A**   Changes in Functions and Structures of States: 8000 B.C.E.–600 C.E.

Alexander's empire stretched from his native Macedonia through most of the Greek peninsula (choice **C**) and south toward Egypt (choice **D**). It extended east as far as the Indus River, including the Persian Empire (choice **B**) and Bactria (choice **E**). However, Alexander did not conquer Arabia, choice **A**, which was largely desert and thus did not present much of motive for him to lead his forces in that direction.

5. **A**   Patterns and Impacts of Interaction: 600 C.E.–1450

Buddhism reached Southeast Asia by two routes. The first Buddhist missionaries sent forth by the Emperor Asoka went to Sri Lanka and then east toward the mainland. This accounts for the prevalence of the older Thervadan Buddhism in modern Myanmar and Thailand. Meanwhile, Buddhists on the Silk Road gradually expanded Mahayana Buddhism into China, where it then diffused to the South. This explains the prevalence of the "younger" form of Buddhism in not only China but also modern Vietnam and Cambodia. Because the missionaries were going east and south, the correct answer is from the west and north.

6. **B**   Cultural and Intellectual Developments: 600 C.E.–1450

Both the Mayan and Egyptian pyramids are still visible today and attract tourists from around the world, making choice **B** the correct answer. The Mayans did not believe that their kings were gods, as in choice **A**, as Egyptians believed of their Pharaoh. While the Mayan Empire was established in roughly the third century B.C.E., as in choice **C**, Egypt had been founded in the third millennia B.C.E. (c. 3000 B.C.E.) Neither believed in monotheism, as indicated in choice **D**, although there was a brief exception in Egypt with the worship of the god Amon. Finally, neither empire, despite remarkable infrastructure, developed the wheel, as choice **E** indicates.

7.   **B**   Patterns and Impacts of Interaction: 600 C.E.–1450

The only motive for a merchant to travel great distances (and assume great risks) is the promise of a great reward. This is true today and was even truer in the period 600 C.E. to 1450. As silks, spices, and pearls were both rare and frequently traded before reaching their final destination, they were almost exclusively luxury items. Choice **B** is the correct answer. While silk was a Chinese contribution, pearls and spices were more likely to come from Japan, India, or Southeast Asia, eliminating choice **A** and choice **D**. Contrary to choice **C**, these goods would be traveling east to west on the Silk Road, not vice versa, and while these goods would have been subject to excise taxes during the Han dynasty as choice **E** states, that empire disappeared centuries before this era began.

8.   **E**   Patterns and Impacts of Interaction: 600 C.E.–1450

This is a bit of a trick question as all of the options presented are true. However, only one option is correct, as only one answer can be deduced from looking at the map. Islam did come to West Africa over these routes, as choice **B** indicates, and many of the merchants were Muslims, as choice **A** indicates, but neither of these facts are discernible from the map. Likewise, Timbuktu was a popular destination as indicated in choice **D**, but the map gives no suggestion that it was more popular than Gao or Jenne or any other city. There is also no indication as to what goods were being traded, as in choice **C**. But because the routes all traverse the Sahara Desert, camels would be (and of course were) very beneficial to those who needed to cross. Choice **E** is the only answer discernible from the map.

9.   **B**   Changes in Functions and Structures of States: 600 C.E.–1450

A turning point in the history of Christianity came with the split of the Church into Eastern and Western branches in 1054. One of the crucial points of disagreement between these two schools in the Church was the use of sacred images, or icons. Within the Eastern portion of the "old" Roman Empire (i.e., Byzantium) there were those who felt icons were sacred (iconodules) and those who were opposed to such graven images (iconoclasts). One point of agreement in the East, however, was that the Patriarch of Rome, also known as the pope, had no business trying to settle the dispute. This, among other political and doctrinal issues, led to the Schism and the division of the Church. None of the other choices mentioned had to deal with such a controversy.

10.   **E**   Impact of Technology and Demography: 600 C.E.–1450

Both the Mongols and Turks had a tremendous impact on the settled regions to which they migrated. The Turks were recruited into the service of the Caliphate, as in choice **B**, and eventually took control, but the Mongols were not. The Turks accomplished their takeover, however, without the advantage of Chinese siege technology, choice **C**, which was something the Mongols had acquired when they attacked China. The Mongols would go on to conquer Russia, but not the Turks, eliminating choice **D**. Some Mongols converted to Islam, as choice **A** indicates, but many others converted to Buddhism or remained loyal to the animistic ways of the steppe. Both groups, however, were pastoralists who attacked and conquered sedentary civilizations, as in choice **E**.

11.   **E**   The Relationship of Change and Continuity: 600 C.E.–1450

The Latin term "Pax" means "peace." This should not be confused with the term "pox" (as in "chicken" or "small") which means a disease—though the terms are pronounced the same way. So in essence, the "Pax Mongolica" can be translated to "Peace of the Mongols," making choice **E** the correct answer. During this time, the Mongol Empire established a high level of security for merchants. As pastoralists, the Mongols had come to rely on and value merchants. Trade supplied the manufactured goods the Mongols had no means of creating on the steppe. Choice **C** may also appear correct, as the Mongols did practice remarkable religious tolerance, but this custom is not referred to as the "Peace of the Mongols." The term is somewhat ironic, however, considering the devastation and terror the Mongols visited upon their enemies.

12.   **E**   Social and Gender Structure: 1450–1750

The term "serf" comes from the Latin "servus," meaning "slave." Yet serfs were not slaves, in the way most people picture those in bondage. Serfs were considered part of the land, in Medieval European society. As such, they could be bought and sold with the land, between powerful feudal lords. The serfs themselves, however, could not be separately bought and sold, unlike slaves. Serfs were often well educated, while slaves almost never received any schooling, eliminating choice **B**. Serfs were often farmers, but they might also practice a trade in the winter months or assist in the work of the castle; slaves could be put to any task, eliminating choice **C**. Serfdom was common all across Europe, which was mostly Christian, whereas slavery was uncommon in Europe, eliminating choices **D** and **E**.

13.   **C**   Patterns and Impacts of Interaction: 600 C.E.–1450

There have been many technological breakthroughs by the Chinese that eventually found their way west. Among these was the ability to make paper, which Muslims acquired from the Chinese at the Battle of Talas River, making choice **C** the correct answer. Gunpowder, choice **A**, first passed to the Mongols and then to Muslims through firsthand experience. Tea, choice **D**, would not have been unknown to the Muslims, although they would have more likely encountered it from Indians or from the Chinese. The magnetic compass, choice **B**, also passed to the Muslims, but probably due to contacts with the Chinese on the Indian Ocean, not at the Battle of Talas River. Silk making, choice **E**, was a closely guarded secret, unknown to Muslims at the time, and would be worthless without silk worms.

14.   **B**   Cultural and Intellectual Developments: 1450–1750

During the age of Copernicus (1473-1543), Christian doctrine included a firm belief in an Earth-centered universe. This contention had its roots in Greek and Roman philosophy, and was apparently supported by physical evidence—the progress of the sun across the sky seemed to logically suggest that the sun passes around the Earth. In addition, an Earth-centered universe supported the fundamental Christian belief that human beings were at the center of God's divine plan. Copernicus's teachings, which contradicted Church teachings, threatened to undermine not only the Church's astronomical beliefs but its overall authority as well. This caused the Church to obstruct the burgeoning Scientific Revolution. Copernicus, a Christian (eliminating choice **A**), did not pursue his findings for fear that they would upset the Church's teachings further than they already had. The theory in no way resembled pagan rites (**C**), conflicted with the pope's findings (**E**), or supported the theories of Martin Luther (**D**), who was actually critical of Copernicus' theory.

15. **B**   Social and Gender Structure: 1450–1750

The children of slaves in the Muslim world were generally not considered slaves themselves, unlike slaves in the New World, which eliminates choice **A**. In the Muslim world, most slaves were more likely to be domestics or members of a harem, whereas in the New World, unskilled labor was typical work, eliminating choice **C**. The fact that Muslim demand for slavery was much less than that of Europe and had a less devastating demographic impact eliminates choice **E**. In neither region were slaves converted to one religion forcibly, as choice **D** indicates. The similarity between the two slave institutions lies in the slave trade itself. In both institutions, human cargo was traded for manufactured goods, making choice **B** the correct answer.

16. **D**   Cultural and Intellectual Developments: 1450–1750

For this question, the quote should help jog the student's memory about Akbar, ruler of Mughal India. If not, the quote suggests that Akbar's syncretic religion sought to combine Hinduism and Islam, which should help eliminate most of the options. Southeast Asia, choice **A**, would have had both, as would India, choice **D**. However, whereas Islam could be found in Persia, choice **B**, and East Africa, choice **E**, Hindus would be very scarce, and neither would likely be found in Russia, choice **C**, leaving choice **A** and **D**. Southeast Asia would also have presented a large percentage of Buddhist citizens for a ruler to consider, and as they're not mentioned, it seems more likely that India, choice **D**, would be (and is) the correct choice.

17. **C**   Cultural and Intellectual Developments: 1450–1750

Prince Henry, better known as "the Navigator," was the son of King Joco of Portugal, born in 1394. His interest in exploration led him to create a "think tank" of mariners, cartographers, astronomers, and anyone else who might be of assistance. As a result of the gathering of experts at Sagres, the Portuguese were the first Europeans to sail down the west coast of Africa, eventually rounding the Cape of Good Hope and entering the Indian Ocean.

18. **B**   Impact of Technology and Demography: 1450–1750

The key difference between the Pilgrims (and many other English colonies in North America) and the settlers in New Spain was that the colonists came as families intending to make a new life, while conquistadors were usually single men looking to get rich and return to Spain. While this did indicate an economic difference between the two colonists, the English were not looking for spices as choice **A** indicates. Of the two, the Spanish were more concerned with proselytizing than were the colonists of Plymouth, (choice **C**). The conquistadors were soldiers, subject to military hierarchy, whereas the English settlers came equipped with ideas of a more democratic form of government, which eliminates choice **E**. Finally, their respective crowns initially ran neither the Pilgrims nor the conquistadors, as choice **D** indicates. Eventually, the Plymouth colony became part of the Massachusetts royal colony, and Spanish viceroys took control in New Spain.

19. **C**   Impact of Technology and Demography: 1450–1750

The demise of the samurai was not official until the Meiji Restoration, but the arrival of gunpowder technology in the 1500s signaled its decline. Bullets could pierce the armor of these skilled warriors, and modern warfare called for massive numbers of troops trained for months, compared to the lifelong devotion of the samurai warrior. These innovations lead to the decline of the samurai and to their distinctive battle dress. Western fashions did become popular toward the end of the nineteenth century, but armor wasn't a fashion statement as much as a practical matter of war, so you can eliminate choice **E**. The Tokuga-was relied on their samurai to keep the order and would not humiliate them by forbidding their armor (choice **D**), although the common Japanese citizen was at times prohibited from owning metal implements. (This was mainly out of fear of revolution and explains the development of wooden weapons such as the Nunchaku.) During the Meiji period, samurai were forbidden to carry their ceremonial swords, which was a humiliation to them. Climate change was not a factor (choice **A**). And while industrialization did occur at the same time as the change in warfare, as choice **B** indicates, it was the latter that doomed the armor.

20.   **D**   Social and Gender Structure: 1450–1750

In the year that Columbus sailed for "India," the Spanish government expelled any Jews who would not convert to Christianity. This followed the completion of the *reconquista*, during which Spanish Catholics expelled the remaining Muslims (Moors) from the south of Spain. Jews and Christians, however, did have religious freedom in the Ottoman Empire, and some were valued members of society. Choice **D** is the correct answer. The era also marks the rise of Spain as a trading power (choice **A**), partly at the expense of the Turks, who were seeing their monopoly on Asian goods disappear as Europeans reached Asia on their own. Spain also increased its status with political marriages, into Britain (Katherine of Aragon) and the Hapsburg Empire, to name two examples. The Ottomans gained terri-tory, but not through marriage, eliminating choice **E**. This indicates the greater status women might attain in Spain (e.g., Queen Isabella) than in Turkey (choice **C**), although some female courtiers were quite influential. And while the sultan did have to consult the council of clerics (the *ulama*), as in choice **B**, he was the official and real ruler of the empire, like the king of Spain.

21.   **B**   The Relationship of Change and Continuity: 1450–1750

European exploration along Africa's Atlantic coast began around this time, as did the trad-ing of slaves to Europeans (choice **A**). Constantinople fell in 1453 (choice **C**), marking the end of the Byzantine Empire and a new high point for the Ottomans. The Renaissance (c. 1300–1600) was at its midpoint (choice **D**), and Kilwa and Great Zimbabwe (on the south-eastern coast of Africa) began their decline (choice **E**). The Yuan (Mongol) dynasty of China, however, answer choice **B**, had fallen in 1368, well before 1450.

22.   **E**   Patterns and Impacts of Interaction: 1450–1750

The voyages of Zheng He were primarily intended to demonstrate the power and grandeur of the Ming Empire. Ambassadors were collected and brought back, along with tribute, to the emperor. While trade was not a primary objective, the fleet was on the lookout for goods not available to the Chinese. In this they were similar to the European explorers, making answer choice **E** the correct answer. Proselytization and colonization were not on the Chinese agenda, as choice **D** indicates. European explorers were hoping to find new lands, new souls, and new wealth (choice **A** and **B**), whereas the Chinese had no such goals. While China had access to silver deposits (choice **C**), especially from Japan, the Europeans were eager to find precious metals to enrich their nations and to use to barter with the Chinese.

23.   **C**   Impact of Technology and Demography: 1750–1914

These two revolutions, like all revolutions, were driven by the lower class—those with the least to lose and the most to gain (choice **C**). In Haiti, slaves outnumbered free men nine to one. In France, the Third Estate (including the poor, middle class, and non-noble rich) made up over 95 percent of the population. Slavery, however, was not a key issue in the French Revolution (choice **A**), nor was the sugar trade (choice **D**). Louis's policies were not an issue for the Haitians (choice **B**), because he had been dethroned already when they began to strive for independence. The Americans offered some moral support to the French (choice **E**), but avoided the situation in Haiti completely—even cutting off trade with the new nation for fear that the slave revolt might spread to the Southern states of the United States.

24. **D**   Patterns and Impacts of Interaction: 1750–1914

In many ways, the Haitian Revolution was inevitable, but the French Revolution certainly went a long way toward making it possible. The cries in Paris of "Liberty, Equality, and Fraternity" were soon inspiring the blacks of Haiti, who lived under brutal conditions, to begin thinking of freedom. Choice **D** is therefore the correct answer. While many Haitians were Catholic, the attacks on the Church by the more radical members of the Third Estate were not a concern for Haitians (choice **E**). Certainly, none of the slaves had any sympathy for the French monarch (choice **C**). Napoleon did land troops in Haiti, only in an effort to regain control of the valuable sugar colony (choice **B**), but the revolution itself was already accomplished. As a result of the failure of French troops to retake Haiti, Napoleon chose to sell the Louisiana Territory to the fledgling United States (choice **A**), although it occurred too late to have an impact on the Haitian revolution. This sale freed Napoleon from having to send troops to defend the region and gave him back some of the needed revenue that was lost along with the independence of Haiti.

25. **C**   Social and Gender Structure: 1750–1914

The tales of Native American and native South African abuses are tragically similar. Europeans drove both from their ancestral lands. In the United States, Native Americans were put on reservations. In South Africa, the Natives Land Act enabled the government to relocate all native South Africans to Bantustans, which were similar to the U.S. reservations. Choice **C** is the best answer. The natives in South Africa were coerced to work in the mines or coffee fields, but Native Americans were seldom given jobs of any kind, which eliminates choice **B**. Neither group had representation of their own in any government structure (choice **D**). (The Bureau of Indian Affairs, for example, was the U.S. government's agency for dealing with "Indian problems," but it didn't necessarily represent the concerns of Native Americans.) Many natives did leave the countries of their origin (choice **E**), but in neither case were there wholesale expulsions. In Africa, the natives were to be a workforce, but there was no need for such a force in America. In both countries, some natives converted to Christianity, as choice **A** indicates, but the zealousness of Europeans to convert them was marginal in comparison to other proselytizing missions, such as the Spanish in South and Central America or Jesuit efforts in Japan and China.

26. **A**   The Relationship of Change and Continuity: 1750–1914

Unlike the Roman Catholic Church, the Anglican Church in Britain did not prevent scientists like Newton and others from pursuing their studies, choice **B**, which eventually would lead to a climate for creating inventions like the steam engine and spinning jenny. The boom in agriculture in England lead to an increase in population, choice **D**, which, thanks to the new technology as well as government policies such as the Enclosure Acts (choice **E**), motivated many rural peoples to immigrate to the cities, just in time to work in the new factories. Because British citizens were freer politically than most other nations (choice **C**), they also expected to have liberties in the economic sector. An additional bonus was the British social norm of leaving inheritance to the oldest son, thereby forcing many younger sons to make their own way in the world. This motivated many young inventors and entrepreneurs to undertake ventures that might not have been necessary in other countries. That leaves choice **A**. The oldest universities in Europe were on the Continent (especially in Italy), and not in Britain.

27. **A** Patterns and Impacts of Interaction: 1750–1914

The Opium Wars left no doubt that the relationship between China and the West had reversed its historical pattern. As far back as Roman times, Europeans had not been able to offer much to the Chinese except precious metals (especially silver). Not until the eighteenth century, when the British began to import opium, did the West have a product to trade for Chinese silk, tea, and other products. As a result of the crushing victory by the British in the Opium Wars, they were awarded Hong Kong—although more fighting continued into the nineteenth century to secure the surrounding areas. Choice **A** is the correct answer. Far from being expelled, as choice **C** indicates, British citizens in China flocked to the new hub of trade. The import of opium continued (choice **B**), as did missionary work (choice **E**), although the latter was not really a factor in the war. All of China did not become a British protectorate as choice **D** suggests, and many other nations had already carved out a "spheres of influence."

28. **B** Changes in Functions and Structures of States: 1750–1914

Italy as a unified nation did not emerge until 1870, and by that point most of Africa had been divided up between the existing European powers, making choice **B** the correct answer. Italy was able to wrest Libya from Ottoman control in 1911, but it lost the Battle of Adowa to native Ethiopians in 1896. All of the other choices are factually incorrect: Italy's Catholicism did not stand in the way of its expansion (choice **D**); Italy did not claim any territories in Asia (choice **A**); Italy's natural resources were not so immense as to preclude conquest, as choice **C** indicates; and there was not constant fighting with the Ottoman Empire, as suggested in choice **E**.

29. **E** Patterns and Impacts of Interaction: 1914–Present

The Central Powers were so named because the Allied Powers flanked them to the east and west. Russia declared war on Austria in defense of their fellow Slavs of Serbia. Germany quickly mobilized against Russia, which sparked the entrance of France and Britain on the side of Russia. That aligned Russia, Serbia, France, and Britain on one side, and Germany and Austria on the other. Turkey also joined the Germans and Austrians, creating a bloc that faced Russia to the east and the French/British forces to the west. Answer **E** is the correct grouping.

30. **C** Social and Gender Structure: 1914–Present

Lucretia Mott and Elizabeth Cady Stanton (choices **A** and **E**) were key leaders of the Seneca Falls Convention, which issued a "Declaration" of rights for women in 1848. Susan B. Anthony's (choice **D**) contributions to the rights of women were recognized the United States when she became the first woman commemorated on American currency (the Susan B. Anthony dollar coin). Emmeline Pankhurst (choice **B**) founded Britain's Women's Social and Political Union, the most renowned of Britain's suffrage advocacy groups. Marie Curie, however, while an inspirational and accomplished woman in a field dominated by men, was not a leader in British or American women's rights movements.

31. **D**   Social and Gender Structure: 1914–Present
Golda Meir (choice **A**) was Prime Minister of Israel from 1969 to 1974. Indira Gandhi (choice **B**) the daughter of Jawaharlal Nehru, was Prime Minister of India from 1966 to 1977, and again from 1980 to 1984. Margaret Thatcher (choice **C**), sometimes called "the Iron Lady" for her stern leadership of Britain, was Prime Minister from 1979 to 1990. Benazir Bhutto (choice **E**) was Prime Minister of Pakistan from 1988 to 1996 and the first female leader of a predominantly Islamic nation. Choice **D**, Aung San Su Ky, is a leader of Myanmar's (Burma) democratic reform movement. She won the Nobel Peace Prize in 1991. Although Su Ky is technically the head of a political party that won election in Myanmar in 1990, she was not allowed by the ruling government to take office.

32. **D**   Patterns and Impacts of Interaction: 1914–Present
Colonial occupation by Europeans often overlooked the ethnic and historical differences between native peoples. Modern Iraq, for example, was created in such a way that it is predominantly Shiite Muslim, with a large Sunni and Kurdish minority. Likewise, Rwanda is predominantly Hutu, with a sizable minority of Tutsi. Tutsis are found in greater numbers in neighboring Burundi and Uganda, suggesting that borders drawn on the basis of historical occupation or ethnicity would be quite different than those left behind by the Germans and Belgians. Choice **D** is the correct answer. While all nations have some minority group (even Japan, choice **A**), not all of them have suffered civil strife as a result. Iran's strife has not been ethnic but religious, eliminating choice **A**. India's problems have had more to do with Hindu-Muslim hostility than ethnicity, eliminating choice **C**. And Mexico and Russia (choice **B**, **C**, and **E**) were not nations whose borders were established by colonization.

33. **C**   Patterns and Impacts of Interaction: 1914–Present
Algeria became a French colony in 1834, although a lengthy resistance lasted until 1847. Along with the rest of French North Africa, Algeria remained a French possession until after World War II. Again, there was a lengthy struggle resulting in the deaths of over a million Algerians and French, but Algeria became fully independent in 1962. The choice of options **A** or **B** would be understandable, as Britain controlled nearby Egypt, and Italy controlled neighboring Libya, but only the French controlled Algeria.

34. **C**   Patterns and Impacts of Interaction: 1914–Present
In October of 1945, the retreating troops of General Chiang Kai-shek occupied the island of Taiwan off the coast of mainland China. There, protected by the United States throughout the Cold War and beyond, Taiwan has grown to become an economic powerhouse. The United States does not technically recognize Taiwan's independence from China (who considers the island to be a part of the People's Republic), but the United States has vigorously opposed any move by the mainland to invade or otherwise inhibit the Taiwanese. A central issue for the region in the twenty-first century will be the fate of capitalist Taiwan on the outskirts of the most populous (and still communist) nation in the world.

35. **A**   Changes in Functions and Structures of States: 1914–Present
One of the constant struggles for Mao Zedong after the revolution was how to keep up the fever pitch of change, reform, and evolution in his country. Thus he created many programs and slogans to try and motivate the masses into action. The Four Olds campaign (choice **E**) was launched in the early 1950s to eliminate old ideas, habits, customs, and culture. In their place, Mao encouraged new ideas with his slogan, "Let a hundred flowers bloom" (choice **D**), in 1957, a campaign followed by the "Great Leap Forward" (choice **C**) program in 1958, in which the government tried to collectivize agriculture so more citizens

could create steel in local mills. However, the steel was of very poor quality and drew few buyers and famine swept the nation. Perhaps as a last gasp to spur the nation, Mao launched the Cultural Revolution (choice **B**) in 1967. The Hundred Schools of Thought, choice **A**, was not a slogan by Mao, but a period of philosophical fervor c. fifth century B.C.E., which included the emergence of the Legalists, Confucians, Mohists, and Taoists as well as the military advisor Sun Tzu.

36. **E**   Impact of Technology and Demography: 1914–Present
There are two keys to answering this question. The first is to understand that a portion of a nation, expressed as a percent, does not equate with "raw" numbers. While there may be a larger percentage of "young" people in Cambodia, there are fewer of them overall, compared with Japan, which has a much larger population. Second, developed nations are industrial, like the United States and Japan, whereas developing nations would be nonindustrial, like Cambodia. Armed with that information, the only possible answer is choice **E**.

37. **B**   Cultural and Intellectual Developments: 8000 B.C.E.–600 C.E.
The Indian emperor Asoka reigned during the Mauryan dynasty (265–238 B.C.E.) Originally a warrior-king, Asoka became disgusted with the horrors of war and converted to Buddhism. He proceeded to erect pillars throughout his realm, especially at places central to the life of the Buddha, which explained his new political/spiritual philosophy. The photo in the question is one of these pillars. Symbolism associated with the pillars includes the occasional reference to the Buddha as a lion, roaring (spreading his message) to the four corners of the world (the lions point in different directions in the photo). The other objects listed in the answer choices were also from the ancient period (except the Lions of Emperor Qin, which are fictional), but are not pictured in the photograph.

38. **D**   The Relationship of Change and Continuity: 8000 B.C.E.–600 C.E.
The period of ancient history c. 600 to 300 B.C.E. is often referred to as the Axial Period because so many philosophical and religious ideas developed during this era. Given these dates, it should be obvious that Christianity is the option that does not fit and is therefore the correct answer. Zoroastrianism, choice **A**, involving a view of the world as a dichotomy between good and evil, began c. 600 B.C.E. The life of the Buddha, choice **B**, was c. 542 to 483 B.C.E. Confucius, choice **C**, also lived during the sixth century B.C.E., while Socrates (469–399 B.C.E.), Plato (427–327 B.C.E.), and Aristotle (384–322 B.C.E.), choice **E**, lived in the final years of the Axial Period.

39. **E**   Cultural and Intellectual Developments: 8000 B.C.E.–600 C.E.
Both Taoism and Confucianism sought to bring order to the chaotic era of Chinese history, known as "the Warring States" period (481–221 B.C.E.) Confucianism sought a grass roots order, based on respect for the key relationships of each individual throughout his or her life. Taoism focused on the order already created by nature, such as the balance between diametrically opposing forces, called "yin" and "yang." Answer choice **E** is the correct answer. Despite this similarity, the two religions were really quite different. Taoism preached against man-made rules, whereas Confucianism stressed the order and civility of human rules and society. Of the two, only Confucianism became a "state" religion or philosophy, as it stressed obedience to the ruler (choice **A**). Confucianism was exported to Japan along with other Chinese cultural traits, but Japan's native Shinto religion was similar enough to Taoism as to minimize the latter's impact in Japan (choice **D**). Buddhism would later join these two "faiths" as a key part of Chinese spirituality and as another Chinese export to Japan.

40. **E**   Patterns and Impacts of Interaction: 8000 B.C.E.–600 C.E.

The Hunas (or White Huns) were a pastoral people from Central Asia who invaded and destroyed the Gupta Empire at the end of the fifth century B.C.E. Like other pastoralists, they were polytheistic (animists) and not too fond of settled peoples. In these traits, they were quite like the Huns, who contributed to the downfall of the Roman Empire. Choice **E** is the correct answer. Both groups also share this characteristic with the Xiongnu, who aided in the collapse of the Han dynasty.

41. **C**   Cultural and Intellectual Developments: 600 C.E.–1450

Contrary to the image some may have of Islam today, many scientific and mathematical advances were made in Islamic lands. Islamic doctors and scientists were particularly interested in optics and the eye (choice **E**), reflecting a long heritage in Mesopotamia for beliefs about the spiritual value of eyes. They compiled many medical books (choice **B**), examined and named the stars (choice **D**), and studied mathematics extensively, including algebra and trigonometry (choice **E**). Of the choices listed, only choice **C** is an advancement not made by Muslims.

42. **D**   Social and Gender Structure: 600 C.E.–1450

Ibn Battuta traveled throughout the Islamic (and non-Islamic) world of the early fourteenth century and recorded his observations. One of the obvious conclusions that can be drawn is that as religions come in contact with new regions and cultures, not only are the regions and cultures changed, but often times, the religions changes as well. The customary easiness with which men and women of Mali mixed would no doubt be shocking to Persians, who were accustomed to very strict religious guidelines regarding contact between men and women. While a region's social order may be changed, it is generally not "destroyed" by the new religion, as choice **E** indicates. The women of Mali (who clearly had more, not less, freedom) were not seen as impious by the Islamic community as a whole, as choices **A** and **C** indicate. While it is true that Islam came to West Africa via the trans-Saharan trade, as choice **B** indicates, this fact is not reflected in the quote.

43. **E**   Patterns and Impacts of Interaction: 600 C.E.–1450

Russia was converted to Christianity by Saint Cyrill (creator of Russia's Cyrillic alphabet) and his brother Methodius. This began the process of cultural diffusion between Byzantium and Russia, which was aided by the trade that flowed down Russia's rivers into the Black Sea and on to Constantinople. The Cyrillic alphabet was just the beginning of an infusion of Byzantine culture into Russian society, as choice **E** correctly states. The other answers do not go far enough to specifically explain why the word *czar* was derived from the Roman word Caesar.

44. **A**   Patterns and Impacts of Interaction: 600 C.E.–1450

The march of the Mongols was possibly the most important event of this time period. During this era, the Mongols captured many cities—some through surrender and others through siege. Peking (Beijing) fell in 1215, followed by Samarkand in 1220. Keiv was captured in 1240 and Baghdad in 1258. Choice **A** is the correct choice. All of the other choices were not true of all of the cities mentioned: Kiev did not suffer from the plague (choice **D**), nor did Marco Polo visit it (choice **E**); neither Peking nor Kiev was a stronghold of Islam (choice **C**); and Kiev was well north of the Silk Road (choice **B**).

45. A Impact of Technology and Demography: 600 C.E.–1450

As terrible as the bubonic plague was, its affects were certainly worse in urban areas than in rural ones. The cosmopolitan nature of cities, drawing merchants (choice **C**), pilgrims (choice **E**), and other travelers of all sorts certainly contributed to the spread of the disease, but the greatest weakness of cities was the close proximity in which people lived, allowing the plague-spreading fleas to infect more people. In rural areas, anyone who contracted the disease was far less likely to come in contact with another person before he or she died. The plague was not a waterborne disease, as option **D** suggests, and although cities were certainly filthy by modern standards (choice **B**), the rural citizens were no more enamored of hygiene than their city cousins.

46. C Patterns and Impacts of Interaction: 600 C.E.–1450

The student who knows that *Swahili* derives from an Arabic word meaning "of the coasts" will have no problem with this question. Arab merchants sailed their dhows down the African coast even before the Prophet's *hijra* to Medina. The frequent contact between these peoples led to the development of Swahili, which mixed Arabic with coastal languages. Choice **C** is the correct choice. While the other choices are factually correct—there were Chinese goods (and occasionally merchants) in East Africa (choice **A**) along with Indonesians (choice **E**) and Indians (choice **B**)—none of these had the continuity of contact necessary to create a new language.

47. A Cultural and Intellectual Developments: 600 C.E.–1450

The mosque of Jenne is one of the most well known architectural sites in West Africa. It symbolizes the spread of Islam across the Sahara by merchants eager to trade for gold and slaves. Mansa Musa's hajj to Mecca in 1324 to 1325 resulted in the immigration of many Islamic scholars and experts to West Africa. While the architectural style is clearly of West African descent, the very presence of a mosque so far from the Islamic heartland speaks volumes about the diffusion between these two cultures.

48. E Patterns and Impacts of Interaction: 600–1450

Although the reading focuses on the spread of the Austronesian-speaking peoples mentioned in choices **A** and **B**, it is illustrative of many other historical events as well. The passage does not imply conquest, which rules out choice **A**, as well as the specific comparison to the Mongols in choice **B**. And, while the reading suggests that trade may have been a motive for the migration of these mariners, it is a big leap to suggest that cultural diffusion happens most often because of trade, as in choice **C**. While the first settlers of the Pacific Islands reached the new lands during the last Ice Age, when ocean levels were lower and more land was exposed, as in choice **D**, the reading does not mention that fact. That leaves the most generic of the options, option **E**, as the right choice.

49. A Patterns and Impacts of Interaction: 1450–1750

The Columbian Exchange resulted in the vast transfer of flora and fauna between the "Old World" and the "New World." In addition, both Europeans and African slaves traveled to the Americas, along with their myriad germs. The Europeans brought horses, as well as sheep and wheat. Maize, however, was a staple of many Native American diets in Central America and Mexico, and was not introduced in the New World by Europeans.

50. B Impact of Technology and Demography: 1450–1750

The native population of the Americas dropped by roughly 90 percent in the centuries immediately following the arrival of Europeans. There were many causes, including warfare with the technologically superior Europeans (choice **C**) and the mistreatment of natives in mines and plantations (choice **A**). By far the biggest killer, however, was the influx of new, European germs. The lack of large domesticated mammals in the New World had prevented the natives from being exposed to animal-related diseases like small-pox and measles, and because Europeans had co-existed with these germs for generations, they had developed greater resistance and were thus much less affected by them. The remaining two choices are factually incorrect.

51. **A**   Patterns and Impacts of Interaction: 1450–1750
The demand for these products drove Europeans to sail uncharted waters along the west coast of Africa and eventually around the globe. Europeans were driven to take these risks because the Ottoman Empire had so effectively monopolized trade with Asia that there were simply no profits to be had by most European merchants. If the Europeans could have managed to cooperate with one another, they could have defeated the Ottomans rather than risk their lives on the sea, but they could never reach such accord, eliminating answer choice **B**. Ironically, the merchants of the Indian Ocean (Muslim and otherwise) were generally not armed and shared in the trade of these and other goods (choice **D**). No one nation or ethnicity—Arab, Chinese, etc.—completely controlled the Indian Ocean trade before the Europeans showed up, which eliminates choice **C**. Some of these products were available in Japan, but none of them were available in abundance (choice **E**).

52. **C**   Changes in Functions and Structures of States: 1450–1750
Europeans supplied African leaders with the weapons (and other manufactured goods) necessary for military and economic success, and in return, the African leaders supplied the Europeans with their enemy prisoners. The modern notion of loyalty to one's race or continent did not exist. Of course, the Europeans didn't just choose sides. They often sup-plied "the enemy" with weapons as well. The notion of slavery was ancient in most Afri-can societies, eliminating choice **D**. The volume of the European slave trade, however, was new and devastating to Africa demographically. The total number of Africans taken in the slave trade to the Americas are usually estimated conservatively around 9 million. Africa did have other resources to trade, as in choice **B**, but the Europeans needed a labor force, which is what made slavery an attractive option. Religion played no part in the decisions of African leaders as choice **A** indicates, other than to try and improve their status with Europeans. There is no evidence to suggest the claims made in choice **E**.

53. **A**   Patterns and Impacts of Interaction: 1450–1750
Most trade is based on getting what you don't have in return for what you do have. This explains all three corners of what was called the Triangular Trade. Africa had slaves and raw materials such as ivory but lacked manufactured goods (eliminating option **B**). Europe had manufactured goods in abundance but needed slaves and raw materials. The colonies could produce raw materials but needed labor and manufactured goods. The map doesn't explain who sailed where. Although the map doesn't disprove this, few African merchants were sailing to the Atlantic on a regular basis, as choice **D** indicates. Likewise, the map doesn't show wind or water currents to explain why ships sailed the routes they did. Wind and water did play a role, but not in the way option **C** suggests. The value and necessity of various items is also not specified, eliminating choice **E**.

54. **E**   Social and Gender Structure: 1450–1750
In some parts of India, a woman who did not have children to raise would (in various ways) commit suicide at her husband's funeral. The belief was that this would provide

good karma and possibly reunite the couple in the next life. Women who did not perform this ritual were socially outcast. Non-Hindu rulers of India (Muslim and European) however, loathed this practice and tried to prevent it to varying degrees. It continues into the present, although quite rarely. All other suggested definitions can be eliminated.

55. **D** Changes in Functions and Structures of States: 1450–1750

The Ottomans were Turks, and their rulers held the title of Sultan. Ottomans also followed the rulings of the *ulama,* or council of religious scholars, who governed from a religious standpoint. While the sultan certainly outranked any other person in the empire, the collective power of the ulama could "check" a sultan and at times participated in replacing sultans who were too liberal. If the ulama removed its support for a sultan, his enemies could move in and depose him without fear of religious repercussions, and possibly with the scholars' blessing. Thus the sultan and the ulama could be said to have ruled the Ottoman Empire together. The term shah usually refers to the rulers of Persia, who were Shi'ia. The caliphs were rulers in the Abbasid Empire—i.e., Arabs. They ruled as kings first, but with some right to engage in religious matters.

56. **E** Patterns and Impacts of Interaction: 1450–1750

Well before 1760, the Japanese had expelled all foreigners except for occasional Dutch missionaries. These missions were conducted on a narrow sandbar called Deshima Island, in Nagasaki harbor. Meanwhile, as of 1759, the Qing dynasty of China had confined foreigners to the southern city of Guangzhou, or Canton. Choice **E** is the correct answer. At this point in history, China and Japan were in similar positions vis-à-vis the Europeans, but that would change in the coming centuries, as Japan adapted to Western ways and China did not.

57. **E** Cultural and Intellectual Developments: 1750–1914

As the gulf between industrialized nations and the rest of the world began to widen, new forms of colonialism began to form. Most important was Neocolonialism, in which an industrialized nation (e.g., the United States) controlled the economy of an otherwise independent nation (choice **E**). Because the investment in the developing nation's economy was so great, the developed nation could threaten to de-invest and the throw the economy into chaos. Thus, while they didn't directly control the economy or the government, the industrialized nation had de facto control of the developing country. Neocolonialism came about mainly in the nineteenth century when industrialized nations were in search of raw materials, as choice **B** suggests. However, this was not always the case, and in multiple-choice questions, "a little wrong is the same as all wrong." Option **E** describes neocolonialism in all situations.

58. **B** Patterns and Impacts of Interaction: 1750–1914

The Meiji Restoration was an attempt by *daimyos* and samurai to change Japan's government, in part so that the nation could modernize along European and American lines. The Young Turks were a group of Turkish intellectuals who saw modernization as the only way to save their nation. In response to the growing hegemony of the industrialized nations, both groups sought change at the highest levels for what might be called nationalist reasons. Unlike the young Turks, the Japanese were successful, which eliminates choice **D**. Many of the Young Turks were exiled. The Japanese reformers were not focused on religion at all, and neither group was supported directly by Europeans, eliminating choices **C** and **E**. Choice **A** is not true of both movements.

59. E   Changes in Functions and Structures of States: 1750–1914

The Sepoy Revolt (also called the Sepoy Mutiny) began when Indians who were employed as soldiers (called *sepoys*) by the British East India Company objected to the use of animal fat on their ammunition cartridges. The result was the slaughter of hundreds of innocent British women and children, and some British men. This was followed by the equally horrific massacre and humiliation of many sepoys. The significance of the event, however, is that it led to direct British control of India. A governor was appointed, the viceroy, on behalf of the Parliament and Queen Victoria. Economics was not an issue, nor were the French (choices **B** and **C**). There was no system of provincial government in place for Hindus to dominate, as choice **D** indicates, although they were the majority religion.

60. D   Impact of Technology and Demography: 1750–1914

The Suez Canal was really just a large trench that connected the Mediterranean Sea to the Red Sea. It was, however, a huge boon to Europeans trying to get to the Indian Ocean, cutting travel time by weeks. The idea was so successful that the French (who had been primarily responsible for its construction) decided that the same could be accomplished by cutting through Central America. The site they finally settled on was in modern Panama, but it proved to be a much more challenging terrain than the deserts of the Suez. Changes in elevation and tropical maladies made the project too difficult for the French, who soon abandoned the task to the Americans, who completed the project. The French also built the Eiffel Tower and the Statue of Liberty, the latter of which was a gift to the United States, but the railways of India (choice **A**) were British, and the Erie Canal (choice **C**) was American, as was the Golden Gate Bridge (choice **B**). The Ho Chi Minh Trail (choice **E**), though located in what had been French Indochina, was developed after 1914, as was the Maginot Line (choice **E**), a string of defenses meant to ward off a German attack on northern France in the World War I. The Straits of Malacca (choice **B**) are a natural occurring feature of Southeast Asia.

61. C   Changes in Functions and Structures of States: 1750–1914

Japan's emergence as a world power in the nineteenth and twentieth centuries, was nothing short of amazing. Prior to Commodore Perry's arrival in 1853, Japan had been isolated. Life was like it had been in 1753 or 1653, in most respects. However, in less than fifty years, Japan modernized and become a force on the international stage. In 1894–1895, Japan defeated China in a war (choice **A**), resulting in the Treaty of Shimonoseki. The treaty gained Taiwan and the Pescadore islands for Japan. In 1904–1905, Japan defeated Russia in the Russo-Japanese War (choice **B**), which resulted in Japan capturing Port Arthur and making Korea a protectorate. Korea became a full colony of Japan (called Chosen) in 1910 (choice **D**). Japan was recognized as a major world power, especially with regard to its naval might, in the Five Power Treaty and Four Power Treaty of 1921–1922 (choice **E**), which included the United States and Britain. These treaties restricted the size of the world's great navies. How they did so is less important than the fact that Japan was among the nations in negotiations. Japan conquered the Philippines (choice **C**) during the World War II, but that was after 1930. Choice **C** is the correct answer.

62. E   Impact of Technology and Demography: 1750–1914

A key part of this question is considering what the graph can tell the reader. The graph does not, for instance, explain why so (relatively) few Asians and Africans were immigrating (choice **D**). American government policy, which was discriminatory, was a large part of the reason, but the graph does not divulge that. Likewise, the graph does not explain where these immigrants entered the country (choice **A**) or how they got here (choice **C**). It also does not distinguish between individual nations such as France or Germany (choice **B**). Thus, while one could argue about the meaning of the term "extensive," choice **E** is the only choice that is not clearly wrong.

63.   **A**   Patterns and Impacts of Interaction: 1750–1914

Many of the earliest British settlers of Australia (c. 1788) were in fact convicts, ordered to serve out their sentences in exile. Many British convicts had previously been sent to Georgia or the Carolinas, but the American Revolution ended that practice. Australia was rich with diamonds, but no one realized this until the late twentieth century. The settlers of Australia, being largely British, were also largely Protestants, which eliminates choice **D**. While Australia did not have significant strategic value for trans-Pacific shipping, Singapore, on the other hand, was valuable because of its location. Situated on the tip of the Malay Peninsula, Singapore controlled the Straits of Malacca as the key British outpost against the Dutch. Choice **A** is the correct answer. While there was a rubber trade in Southeast Asia, as choice **B** indicates, Singapore's value was primarily its location and role as trade center for all Asian goods. Japan did conquer Singapore during the Second World War, but previously it had been under the control of the British, eliminating choice **C**. Singapore is in the Pacific Ocean, near, but not in, the Indian Ocean, as choice **E** states.

64.   **D**   Patterns and Impacts of Interaction: 1914–2005

The 1980s saw the United States still embroiled in the Cold War and the struggle to combat communism. America saw the Sandinistas of Nicaragua and the left-wing opposition to the Salvadoran government as dominoes in the global game of containment. In short, America feared another Cuba, and choice **D** states this clearly. Oil and fruit issues were not significant (choice **E**), although fruit companies had played a large role in earlier U.S. foreign policy for the region, and neither were these actions tied to the Monroe Doctrine, as choice **B** indicates. While the leaders of Nicaragua and El Salvador were dictators at times (choice **C**), the motivation on the part of the United States to intervene was more Cold War strategy than personal. At the time, the United States was not desperate to secure oil reserves in Central America, as choice **A** states.

65.   **B**   Social and Gender Structure: 1914–Present

Both Turkey and Saudi Arabia are overwhelmingly Muslim, yet the women of these two nations have very different lives. Saudi women are not allowed to vote or drive. When in public, they must be dressed according to the rules established by the "religious police" (*mutawwa'in*). Turkish women, however, live in a very secular nation, with full rights including voting and driving. While Turkey has some Islamic-based laws, it has also forbid female students at the national university from covering their heads, thus signaling the government's determination not to become an "Islamic state" like Iran or, arguably, Saudi Arabia. Choice **B** is the correct answer. All other choices misstate the rights of women in each country.

66.   **B**   Patterns and Impacts of Interaction: 1914–Present

The view of the UN Security Council today may seem a bit odd. For example, the world's largest democracy (India) is not included, nor is any Muslim nation. Two major economic powers, Japan and Germany, are not included because they were defeated in the Second World War. The victors in the War, the United States, France, Britain, Russia (formerly the Soviet Union), and China have the ability to veto any action by the Security Council. Of the choices, only choice **B** lists three of these nations.

67. **D**   Changes in Functions and Structures of States: 1914–Present

The genocides of the Soviet Union under Stalin and the Cambodian Khmer Rouge were only similar in their communist heritage, as choice **D** states. Stalin's goals were largely political, whether eliminating suspected political opponents or bending the Ukrainians to his will; his motives were not religious, ethnic, or agrarian (choices **A**, **B**, and **C**). The Khmer Rouge claimed to be trying to make an idyllic, agrarian state by evacuating the cities and forcing everyone into collectivized labor. While Catholics were suspected as being pro-Western, those killed by the Cambodians were also Cambodian. The Chinese communists directed neither episode (choice **E**).

68. **D**   Impact of Technology and Demography: 1914–Present

All five of the nations have very large populations, but the People's Republic of China is by far the largest. China has had a policy of limiting couples to only one child. Violation of this policy involves fines and (in extreme cases) sterilization. However it was India, under Prime Minister Indira Gandhi, which created a policy of voluntary sterilization to try and reduce population growth. The policy was not very popular, perhaps explaining why other nations have not been eager to follow suit. Choice **D** is the correct answer.

69. **A**   Cultural and Intellectual Developments: 1914–Present

The Taliban received a great deal of negative attention from a wide range of people, governments, and organizations during its short reign. It restricted civil liberties and civil rights, curtailed women's rights, and destroyed works of art that were considered unacceptable by the Taliban's staunchly conservative interpretation of the Qur'an. What caused UNESCO to protest, however, was the destruction of Buddhist statues, dating back to approximately the fourth century. These statues, each over twelve stories high, dated back to a time before Islam itself had existed. Choice **A** is the correct answer. Today, both the statues and the Taliban are gone.

70. **A**   Cultural and Intellectual Developments: 1914–Present

The term *Bollywood* refers to the Indian film industry, centered in Bombay. Some of the movies are distributed in the United States, and increasingly Indians are gaining prominence in the global film market. The significance of this is the extra voice it adds to the cacophony that is the global culture. While the American media dominate much of global culture, Japan, India, and other nations are also contributors. Bollywood films are more likely to be Indian-affirming, thus not upsetting language trends (choice **D**). But the movies are not generally politically (choice **B**) or religiously (choice **E**) motivated, nor do they make up a huge segment of India's vast economy (choice **C**). Choice **A** is the correct answer.

SECTION II: FREE-RESPONSE EXPLANATIONS

Question 1: Document Based Question

Sample DBQ Essay Response

Conditions in many African nations today are truly tragic. HIV/AIDS is ravaging the populace. War has afflicted most of the continent, and debt to other nations prevents African nations from solving many of their own problems. While a few of these problems can be traced back to the era of European colonialism, these issues cannot entirely be blamed on Europe. In other words, the statement in the question above is false—even if Africa's financial and civil conflicts can be blamed on Europe, Africa's AIDS crisis is not Europe's fault.

The AIDS crisis in Africa has recently approached epidemic levels in some regions. Southernmost Africa is losing people by the thousands according to the United Nations (Document 2). This has not only created the demographic problems associated with plague and pestilence, but it is destroying Africa for generations to come. Children of AIDS victims are forced to raise themselves (Document 5) or fall into unscrupulous hands (see next paragraph). But Europeans didn't cause or create AIDS. If anything, their membership in the UN is helping to fight the disease. The African AIDS crisis is a distinctly African problem. One document that would be an interesting addition to those provided might be the diary of a citizen of a southern African nation. He would probably have no idea how Europeans might be responsible for AIDS in Africa.

The problem of civil war, however, may have some culpability for Europe. When European rulers created their colonies in Africa, they did so without regard for ethnic or tribal geography. This led to nations with sizable minorities of traditional rivals. The size and breadth of warfare in Africa is evident from Document 6. However, Document 6 may not be a very reliable document. It comes from a book titled Africa's Wars and the Prospects for Peace. *If this book detailed only a few wars, it wouldn't be a very compelling book. Thus, the author may have a reason to exaggerate. The horrific Document 4, however, backs up Document 6. The use of children as soldiers is not unique to Africa, but it supports the fact that war is a grievous problem for much of the continent. Even if the wars in Africa are Europe's fault, however (which is not made clear by the documents), the use of children soldiers certainly is not.*

Finally, there is the debt issue. African nations are generally poor and are at least millions if not billions of dollars in debt to the world's wealthier countries. Part of the reason for this debt is that when Europeans colonized Africa (mostly in the nineteenth century) they ran the government, economy, and most business themselves. This deprived Africa of a native administrative ruling class. When the Europeans left, Africa had no financiers or trained governors, so, not surprisingly, the economies of Africa are generally in shambles. However, the documents do little to support this notion. Document 1 is from an organization that tries to motivate people to help Africa. Although this is a worthy cause, the organization might have a motive to exaggerate or bend the truth. Document 3 also seems to support the debt issue, but how much expertise does the singer Bono really have on this topic? When these documents are viewed alongside Document 7, they seem even less reputable. U.S. Treasury Secretary O'Neill suggests that there is plenty of money coming to help Africa ($300 million) but that it is being misspent. Although the Europeans may have begun this problem by not training or involving any natives in their colonial government, they do seem to be trying to help. The root of the problem (from the only reliable source) *seems to be uniquely African. An additional document that would support this claim would be the point of view of someone from another developing nation NOT in Africa (Central America or Southeast Asia). This document—perhaps a chart—would show that while Europeans colonized many nations, only those in Africa are falling so far behind the rest of the world.*

In short, the statement is false because Africa's AIDS is not Europe's fault, even if the financial and civil conflicts are. HIV/AIDS is ravaging the populace. War has afflicted most of the continent. Finally, debt to other nations prevents African nations from solving many of their own problems. Although tragic, these conditions are not largely of Europe's doing.

DBQ Essay Discussion

The DBQ is scored on a 9-point scale along the following guidelines:

1. Provides an acceptable thesis—1 point
2. Uses all or all but one of the documents—1 point
3. Shows an understanding of all or all but one of the cited documents—1 point
4. Supports thesis with evidence from the documents—1 point
5. Analyzes point of view in at least two documents—1 point
6. Addresses question by grouping documents in a certain way, depending on the question—1 point
7. Identifies one type of additional document—1 point.

To earn the remaining two points, the essay must expand beyond these "basic" points, including analyzing the point of view of all documents, bringing in many additional documents and outside information, and showing especially insightful analysis. The sample essay provided is an example of a high-scoring essay that accomplishes many of these things. Let's look at it in depth.

The Thesis Statement: The first point of every AP World History scoring rubric comes from the thesis. Thus, the first goal of every student should be to draft an introductory paragraph with an adequate thesis. The introductory paragraph is crucial as it explains what you are going to address in your essay. It sets the tone. You begin generally and then become more specific until you conclude by stating your argument in a concise statement. Here is the thesis paragraph from the sample essay, with the thesis statement underlined:

> **Thesis Paragraph:**
> *Conditions in many African nations today are truly tragic. HIV/AIDS is ravaging the populace. War has afflicted most of the continent, and debt to other nations prevents African nations from solving many of their own problems. While a few of these problems can be traced back to the era of European colonialism, these issues cannot entirely be blamed on Europe. <u>In other words, the statement in the question above is false; even if Africa's financial and civil conflicts can be blamed on Europe, Africa's AIDS epidemic is not Europe's fault.</u>*

In coming to a conclusion about what your thesis will be, you'll have looked over the documents, evaluating their main ideas and their points of view. Try to put them into three groups that can be the main points for your thesis. (For example, in this DBQ, Documents 2 and 5 are about AIDS; Documents 6 and 4 are about war; Documents 1, 3, and 7 discuss the debt issue.) It may be possible (or necessary) to use one document more than once, if it's long enough to have more than one relevant main idea. But it is imperative that you try to use as many documents as possible. The ideal would be to use them all. Use the documents to support your thesis by continually tying each document back to your argument in the supporting paragraphs. These paragraphs compose the main body of your essay and should always reinforce your thesis statement. Let's look at a supporting paragraph from the sample essay:

> **Supporting Paragraph:**
>
> *The AIDS crisis in Africa has recently approached epidemic levels in some regions. Southernmost Africa is losing people by the thousands according to the United Nations (Document 2). This has not only created the demographic problems associated with plague and pestilence, but it is destroying Africa for generations to come. Children of AIDS victims are forced to raise themselves (Document 5) or fall into unscrupulous hands (see next paragraph). But Europeans didn't cause or create AIDS. If anything, their membership in the UN is helping to fight the disease. The African AIDS crisis is a distinctly African problem. One document that would be an interesting addition to those provided might be the diary of a citizen of a southern African nation. He would probably have no idea how Europeans might be responsible for AIDS in Africa.*

This paragraph uses the documents to support the essay's thesis. The writer has not simply summarized the documents but used them in a very specific way. Be sure to write an essay in which the documents support your point, not an essay in which you try to support the documents.

The two most important parts of a DBQ essay are the thesis paragraph and the supporting (body) paragraphs. However, there are two remaining sections that will earn you the maximum number of points on the DBQ: Additional Documents statement and the Point of View (POV) statements.

Additional Documents Statement: Another component of an AP World History DBQ is the "additional documents" statement. In this case, the student must act like a historian and consider what type of information NOT provided by the documents would help to answer the question. It is also a good idea, that the "additional documents" supports your thesis and your arguments. Since you get to create it yourself, you may as well have it add to your point. Note how the paragraph above also shows the Additional Documents Statement. Consider if there are voices not being heard, such as that of women or men, slaves, rulers, nobles, or colonists. Also, consider if there are types of information that would help, such as demographics or election returns. If there were a chart that accompanied these documents, what might it show?

It is a good idea to add this statement to whichever of your paragraphs references the fewest documents from those provided. What kind of evidence would help prove your thesis? Whose point of view is not represented? Also, be sure when discussing this "fictional" document that you explain not only what it might say, but also how it would help prove your thesis. Let's look at the second Additional Documents Statement from the sample essay: "An additional document that would support this claim would be the point of view of someone from another developing nation NOT in Africa (Central America or Southeast Asia). This document—perhaps a chart—would show that although Europeans colonized many nations, only those in Africa are falling so far behind the rest of the world." The additional document is not only introduced, but its impact is thoroughly explained.

Point of View Statements: An additional way you need to support your thesis is by evaluating the reliability of at least three of the documents. Some documents are less reliable than others because the author is either knowingly or unknowingly misleading the reader. This is called analyzing the document's point of view. Consider the following example:

> **Point of View Paragraph:**
>
> *Finally, there is the debt issue. African nations are generally poor and are millions if not billions of dollars in debt to the world's wealthier countries. Part of the reason for this debt is that when Europeans colonized Africa (mostly in the nineteenth century) they ran the government, economy, and most business themselves. This deprived Africa of a native administrative ruling class. When the Europeans left, Africa had no financiers or trained governors, so, not surprisingly, the economies of Africa are generally in shambles. However, the documents do little to support this. Document 1 is from an organization that tries to motivate people to help Africa. Although this is a worthy cause, the organization might have a motive to exaggerate or bend the truth. Document 3 also seems to support the debt issue, but how much expertise does the singer Bono really have on this topic? When these documents are viewed alongside Document 7, they seem even less reputable. U.S. Treasury Secretary O'Neill suggests that there is plenty of money coming to help Africa ($300 million) but that it is being misspent. Although the Europeans may have begun this problem by not training or involving any natives in their colonial government, they do seem to be trying to help. The root of the problem (from the only reliable source) seems to be uniquely African.*

If a document seems to disagree with your thesis, try to discredit it by attacking its reliability. If a document supports your thesis, try to clarify why it is a document with great reliability. In Document 7, the speaker is U.S. Treasury Secretary Paul O'Neill. He is likely to be someone acutely aware of the amount of money given to Africa, and how that money could or should be spent.

Conclude your essay by restating your thesis. Remember, do not put any new information in your conclusion paragraph. Let the conclusion paragraph restate your thesis and your main points so they're clear to the reader. The conclusion paragraph's purpose is just that—to conclude!

Question 2: Change over Time

Sample Essay Response

The Central American and Caribbean region would be scarcely recognizable today to someone who lived in the region six hundred years ago. Most of the natives are long gone—mostly to illness. In their place are the descendants of Africans and Europeans who have mostly settled in cities rather than in the jungles and countryside. Urbanization, immigration, and disease all had a huge impact on the Central American and Caribbean regions and changed the region in ways a native living in 1400 could scarcely imagine.

The peoples of Central America and the Caribbean c. 1400 were mostly hunters and gatherers living in small villages. The notable exception was the Aztec empire of Mexico, founded c. 1100 C.E. The Aztecs were the cultural heirs of several previous cultures, including the Maya, Olmec, and Toltec peoples. The Aztecs ruled from several large cities dominating villages of other tribes in the countryside. But all that changed with the arrival of

Columbus on the island of Hispaniola in 1492. Columbus, Cortez, and the other conquistadors exposed the natives to pathogens they had never been exposed to before. These diseases, like smallpox and measles, had come to humans via domesticated mammals, of which the Europeans had many (for millennia) and the Native Americans had none. The population of natives in 1450 was roughly in the millions (accurate numbers aren't known). By 1750, less than 10 percent were probably left. By then, disease had also affected Europeans, such as the French troops trying to reclaim Haiti for Napoleon, c. 1802, who died in huge numbers from malaria. In 1914 disease was still an issue. French workers on the Panama Canal suffered so mightily from tropical diseases native to the New World that the French gave up the Canal. But medical science was beginning to understand how microbiology worked and disease was decreasing as a demographic force.

Immigration shows an opposite pattern. In 1450, there were no immigrants to the region. Of course this would change within fifty years as Europeans began to trickle in. These initial immigrants were few but incredibly significant to the region. They brought new germs but also Christianity, new animals (horses and cows etc.) and new plants (wheat and sugar etc.) As the natives of the region died, the Europeans began to replace them with African slaves. Thus, by 1750 Africans (perhaps as many as 10 million; estimates vary) and their descendants far outnumbered the Europeans and their descendants. On Haiti, for example, there were roughly 500,000 slaves in 1790 versus 40,000 whites and 30,000 "freed" peoples of color. The end of slavery in the early nineteenth century altered the immigration pattern yet again as indentured slaves from China and India were transported (mostly to the Caribbean) to work the sugar fields. These immigrants numbered in the tens of thousands, which was enough to make them a sizable chunk of the population of these areas. Despite these changes, there were a few things that remained constant. Native Americans continued to be present, although their numbers dwindled. Even in 1914, they did exist, often poor and oppressed by a social system that still discriminated against them. Many lived in villages that were modern in many ways but not much larger than those of their ancestors.

The village had been the norm in 1450. The Aztec capital of Tenochtitlan had roughly 200,000 people when Cortez arrived in 1521. This made it a city comparable to all but the largest cities in Europe. Most other cities in the region, however, (Chichen Itza and Tikal) had fallen into disuse, and there were few cities overall. By 1750, Mexico City had emerged as an important administrative center. Other cities included Panama, Acapulco, Santo Domingo, and Cartagena. The Industrial Revolution and improving health care helped increase the population in the Central American/Caribbean region as the year 1914 approached. Increasing numbers of people moved to the region's growing cities, including the capitals of nations that had become independent in the preceding decades, like Managua, San Salvador, and Port-au-Prince. These changes in demography in many ways reflected demographic changes worldwide during this era. Europeans spread around the world through colonialism. The Industrial Revolution exacerbated the differences between the Europeans and others, leading to increased urbanization for the millions of "new" immigrants from Europe and Africa.

In summary, Central America and the Caribbean changed drastically from 1450 to 1914 due to diseases, immigration, and urbanization. Most of the natives disappeared, generally to illness. In their place were the descendants of Africans and Europeans. Finally, the number of cities was much greater than it had been. The Central American and Caribbean region would scarcely be recognizable today to someone who lived there six hundred years ago.

Change over Time Essay Discussion

The Change over Time (COT) essay is scored on a 9-point scale along the following guidelines:

1. Provides an acceptable thesis—1 point
2. Addresses all parts of the question—2 points
3. Supports the thesis with evidence—2 points
4. Uses historical context to show the changes over time—1 point

To earn the remaining three points, the essay must expand beyond these "basic" points, including addressing all parts of the question equally, bringing in outside information, and showing especially insightful analysis. The sample essay provided is an example of a high-scoring essay that accomplishes many of these things.

Most AP World History students consider the Change over Time Essay to be the hardest of the three essays. Not only do you have to address how something has or hasn't changed, but you also need to offer evidence of that change in at least three different time periods. The challenge is daunting, but there are some tips that can help.

Thesis Paragraph: As always, the battle can be won or lost with the thesis. A non-existent thesis will deprive you of one of the basic core points in the rubric and end any chance you might have had of getting extended bonus points. The thesis for a COT essay, like all AP World History essays, needs to have an argument and some indicators of your main support points. Think of the thesis as: Thesis = Argument + A + B + C, where A, B and C represent your three key points of change or continuity. Let's look at the thesis paragraph from the sample essay:

Thesis Paragraph:
The Central American and Caribbean region would be scarcely recognizable today to someone who lived in the region six hundred years ago. Most of the natives are long gone—mostly to illness. In their place are the descendants of Africans and Europeans, who have mostly settled in cities rather than in the jungles and countryside. <u>Urbanization, immigration, and disease all had a huge impact on the Central American and Caribbean regions and changed the region in ways a native living in 1400 could scarcely imagine.</u>

In this thesis paragraph, the thesis statement has been underlined. This is the main point of the essay, and all supporting paragraphs will support this main point. Notice also how the three ways to support the argument are clearly stated. Each of these statements will be a supporting paragraph.

Supporting Paragraphs: Now that we know what we are trying to prove in our essay we can move on to the supporting paragraphs. Each paragraph will be tied clearly back to the main point. In addition, each paragraph must give specific information with as many details as possible. The details included in each paragraphs will make your argument stronger. Let's look at a supporting paragraph from the sample essay. Note that the examples of specific evidence have been underlined.

Paragraph 1:
Immigration shows an opposite pattern. In 1450, there were no immigrants to the region. Of course this would change within fifty years as Europeans began to trickle in. These initial immigrants were few but incredibly significant to the region. They brought new germs but also <u>Christianity</u>, new animals (<u>horses</u>

and cows etc.) and new plants (<u>wheat and sugar</u> etc.) As the natives of the region died, the Europeans began to replace them with African slaves. Thus, by 1750 Africans (<u>perhaps as many as 10 million</u>; estimates vary) and their descendants far outnumbered the Europeans and their descendants. On Haiti, for example, there were roughly <u>500,000</u> slaves in 1790 versus <u>40,000</u> whites and <u>30,000</u> "freed" peoples of color. The end of slavery in the early nineteenth century altered the immigration pattern yet again as indentured slaves from <u>China and India</u> were transported (mostly to the Caribbean) to work the <u>sugar fields</u>. These immigrants numbered in the <u>tens of thousands</u>, which was enough to make them a sizable chunk of the population of these areas.

Now read the same paragraph without the specific information:

Paragraph 2:

Immigration shows an opposite pattern. In 1450, there were no immigrants to the region. Of course this would change within fifty years, as Europeans began to trickle in. These initial immigrants were few but incredibly significant to the region. They brought not only new germs, but also new religions, new animals, and new plants. As the natives of the region died, the Europeans began to replace them with African slaves. Thus, by 1750 Africans and their descendants far outnumbered the Europeans and their descendants. On Haiti, for example, there were many more slaves in 1790 than whites and "freed" peoples of color. The end of slavery in the early nineteenth century altered the immigration pattern yet again as indentured servants were transported (mostly to the Caribbean). These immigrants were so numerous as to make them a sizable chunk of the population of these areas.

Paragraph 2 still supports the thesis and offers a direct and relevant comparison. But because it lacks specific evidence, it is inferior to the paragraph from the sample essay. This is of course the great challenge to students—"how much specific evidence do I need?" There is no definitive answer, and students must also balance the need for specifics against the fact that there is a limited amount of time with which to work. A good rule of thumb is to try and include at least three or four specific points in each of your three paragraphs.

Another key issue for students to remember is the need to show change over time by addressing the topic's beginning, ending, and middle or turning point. A common error is for students to only address the beginning and end without any middle point, and therefore there is no analysis of how or why the change occurred. Imagine, for example, that you had to write an essay about how you had or hadn't changed since you were a year old. Would it tell a reader very much if you said something like, "I used to crawl around, but now I can run on the school track team"? How did that happen? At what point did you acquire this skill? Be sure to include a "middle" or turning point in each paragraph where you discuss how an element of change or continuity has affected your thesis topic.

Finally, do not put any new information in your conclusion paragraph. Let the conclusion paragraph re-state your thesis and your main points so they're clear to the reader.

Question 3: Comparison

Sample Essay Response

Society cannot function without both men and women, yet since the earliest times, most societies' religions have given men higher status than women. This is true of Judaism as well as Buddhism, and both religions view women similarly with regard to their place in society. Likewise, they both have only minimal regard for the role of women in the practice of the faith. They differ, however, in terms of their prospects for women in an afterlife. In brief, Judaism and Buddhism have similar outlooks regarding women's social and clerical roles but differing views on their spiritual status.

Judaism is one of the oldest faiths still in practice, dating to c. 1700 B.C.E. Judaism was the first monotheistic faith at that time. The story of Judaism has been one of a small group of people trying to retain their covenant with their god while besieged (literally and figuratively) by the outside world. Buddhism wasn't "born" until a millennia after Judaism (c. 533 B.C.E.) when the (then) Hindu prince Siddhartha Gautama found Enlightenment. While Buddhism has since spread to China, Japan, Korea, and Southeast Asia, it virtually disappeared in its native India. Despite these differences in origin, both faiths have similar views on women in society. Jews are commanded to "honor they father and mother." The role of the mother is crucial in Judaism, and Jewish heritage is traced through mothers. Jewish women have also had property and civil rights, but have been separated from men in the synagogue. Generally, however, Jewish women have had more status than women in most other societies. Likewise, Buddhist women, while not viewed as equals to men, certainly had more status than Hindu or Confucian women. There was no sati (ritual suicide at a husband's funeral) among Buddhists, and women could divorce and remarry (but they could not have multiple spouses like men). Also, Buddhism doesn't stress having sons. This increases the value of girls. In Buddha's directions to married persons, there are directions to both wives and husbands.

Judaism and Buddhism are also similar in their regard for women in the faith. Jewish women cannot become rabbis and aren't counted in the minimum number of faithful needed to recite certain prayers in synagogue. While there have been important women in Judaism, such as Sarah (wife of the founder, Abraham), Rachel, Rebecca, and Moses' sister Miriam, in general Judaism is patriarchal (based around men) and doesn't offer women much of a place in clergy-related affairs. Buddhism doesn't offer much of a role either. Women can become members of the sangha (monastic community) as nuns, or bhikkunis, but are not regarded as highly as the male monks. And although, as with Judaism, there have been important women in Buddhism—including Buddha's mother Queen Maya, his wife Yashodhara, and his aunt—and despite generally preaching equality, Buddhism doesn't offer much of a place for women. The Buddha himself was reluctant to let them become nuns.

Finally, there is an area in which the two religions disagree. Judaism offers women the same option in the afterlife as men. There is no proscription against women going to heaven after death, and in this regard, men and women are equal. Buddhism, however, "discriminates" against women in that being a woman is considered a worse incarnation than being a man. It is assumed that someone is a woman because of "bad" karma in a previous life. However, women can attain merit and Enlightenment on their own. Buddhism is a religion about individual effort toward salvation, and women can make that effort. Thus, in the big picture, women in Judaism and Buddhism were in a better position overall than most women of other faiths. It is difficult to generalize over centuries, varying regions, and even divisions within the faiths, but Jewish and Buddhist women would seem to have had an edge over Hindu and Confucian women.

In conclusion, Judaism and Buddhism have similar outlooks regarding women's social and "clerical" roles but differing views on their "cosmic" status. Judaism and Buddhism view women similarly with regard to their place in society. Likewise, they both have only minimal regard for the role of women in the practice of the faith. They differ, however, in terms of their prospects for women in an afterlife. Since earliest times, most societies have favored men and most religions have given men higher status than women, yet a society needs both to survive.

Comparison Essay Discussion

The Comparison Essay is scored on a 9-point scale along the following guidelines:

1. Provides an acceptable thesis—1 point
2. Addresses all parts of the question—2 points
3. Supports the thesis with evidence—2 point
4. Makes one or two direct comparisons—1 point

To earn the remaining three points, the essay must expand beyond these "basic" points, including addressing all parts of the question equally, relating comparisons to a larger global context, bringing in outside information, and showing especially insightful analysis. The sample essay provided is an example of a high-scoring essay that accomplishes many of these things. Let's look at it in depth.

The Thesis Paragraph: The first point of every AP World History rubric comes from the thesis. Thus, the first goal of every student should be to draft an introductory paragraph with an adequate thesis. Let's look at the thesis paragraph from the sample essay:

> **Thesis Paragraph:**
> *Society cannot function without both men and women, yet since the earliest times, most societies' religions have given men higher status than women. This is true of Judaism as well as Buddhism, and both religions view women similarly with regard to their place in society. Likewise, they both have only minimal regard for the role of women in the practice of the faith. They differ, however, in terms of their prospects for women in an afterlife. <u>In brief, Judaism and Buddhism have similar outlooks regarding women's social and clerical roles but differing views on their spiritual status.</u>*

The thesis statement has been underlined. This introductory paragraph tells the reader what the argument is ("Judaism and Buddhism have similar outlooks on social and clerical roles for women but differing views on their spiritual status") and gives a glimpse of the direction the rest of the essay will take. Each of the three key points (social, clerical, and spiritual status) will become the topic of one of the body paragraphs.

Comparison Paragraphs: The second point of the rubric comes from addressing all parts of the question, though they need not be addressed equally. In this case, a comparison of two religions in regards to women's status must be made, involving similarities and differences. It is vital that students NOT simply discuss one of the two religions, or that they only be discussed briefly. This is where the fourth point of the rubric comes in. To say that Judaism and Buddhism are similar is fine, but you must offer proof. Thus, it is vital to actually know specifics and incorporate them into the body of the essay. Whenever possible, note specific names of people or places and the dates when things happened. Try to utilize vocabulary that is connected with the topic. The more specific you can be, the better. In the paragraph below, each of the specific pieces of information has been underlined:

Comparison Paragraph:

Judaism and Buddhism are also similar in their regard for women in the faith. Jewish women cannot become <u>rabbis</u> and aren't counted in the minimum number of faithful needed to recite certain prayers in <u>synagogue</u>. While there have been important women in Judaism, such as Sarah (<u>wife of the founder, Abraham</u>), <u>Rachel, Rebecca, and Moses' sister Miriam</u>, in general Judaism is <u>patriarchal</u> (based around men) and doesn't offer women much of a place in clergy-related affairs. Buddhism doesn't offer much of a role either. Women can become members of the <u>sangha</u> (monastic community) as nuns, or <u>bhikkunis</u>, but are not regarded as highly as the male monks. And although, as with Judaism, there have been important women in Buddhism, including Buddha's mother <u>Queen Maya</u>, <u>his wife Yashodhara, and his aunt,</u> and despite generally preaching equality, Buddhism doesn't offer much of a place for women. The Buddha himself was reluctant to let them become nuns.

Look at the same paragraph without the underlined terms, and you should see the difference:

Comparison Paragraph 2:

Judaism and Buddhism are also similar in their regard for women in the faith. Jewish women cannot become leaders and aren't counted in the minimum number of faithful needed to recite certain prayers. While there have been some important women in Judaism, in general Judaism is based around men and doesn't offer women much of a place in clergy-related affairs. Buddhism doesn't offer much of a role either. Women can become members of the monastic community as nuns but are not regarded as highly as the male monks. And while, as with Judaism, there have been important women in Buddhism, including Buddha's mother, and despite generally preaching equality, Buddhism doesn't offer much of a place for women. The Buddha himself was reluctant to let them become nuns.

Both paragraphs show the comparison of the two religions, and although Paragraph 2 still supports the thesis and offers a direct and relevant comparison, it lacks specific evidence—it is inferior to the paragraph excerpted from the sample essay. A good rule of thumb is to try and include at least three or four specific points in each of your three paragraphs.

Historical Substantiation: The third point of the rubric is often the most difficult for students. It's one thing to say things were similar or different; it's quite another to offer proof, known in AP parlance as "historical substantiation." Let's again look at the paragraph cited above. Read the following statements and determine which you think would be most effective in this essay.

- Judaism and Buddhism are similar in their regard for women in the faith.
- Judaism and Buddhism are similar in their regard for women in the faith. Jewish women cannot become rabbis.
- Judaism and Buddhism are similar in their regard for women in the faith. Jewish women cannot become rabbis and aren't counted in the minimum number of faithful needed to recite certain prayers in synagogue. Buddhism doesn't offer much of a role either. Women can become members of the *sangha* (monastic community) as nuns, or *bhikkunis*, but are not regarded as highly as the male, monks.

Obviously, the third statement is the best of the bunch. The key is not its length but the specific evidence it cites. It backs up the idea (Judaism and Buddhism are similar) with examples (rabbis and nuns). The first statement above is woefully inadequate, and the second is not much better. The secret is in the details included in the essay. This is where the actual comparing of similarities and differences takes place, and also where the "proof" that the AP graders are looking for can be found.

Finally, a word about the conclusion paragraph: a good writer not only signals where he or she is going with an introductory paragraph and thesis but restates the thesis and main points at the end of the essay. This will remind the reader of what you were saying in case you (or they) "wandered off" during the writing/reading. Begin by restating the thesis, as it's your central argument. Then restate your key points. Do not include any new information in this paragraph. If there was information that could have supported your ideas, it should be up in the body of your essay.

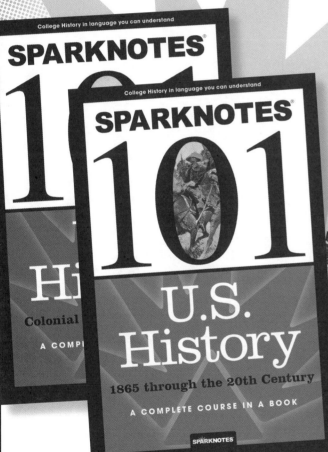